DK

.L

TOP10
LISBON

TOMAS TRANÆUS

D0183905

Top 10 Lisbon Highlights

The Top 10 of Everything

DK | Penguin
Random
House

CONTENTS

Lisbon
Area by Area

Streetsmart

Within each Top 10 list in this book, no hierarchy of quality or popularity is implied. All 10 are, in the editor's opinion, of roughly equal merit.

Front cover and spine An iconic tram in the historic streets of Lisbon, Portugal
Back cover Lisbon's skyline as seen from across the Tejo estuary in Almada
Title page The rooftops of Alfama, Lisbon's oldest district

Welcome to
Lisbon

Lisbon is a city of superlatives: the most westerly capital in mainland Europe, one of the sunniest, one of the least expensive and, draped over a series of hills facing the Tejo estuary, surely one of the most impressively located. With Eyewitness Top 10 Lisbon, it's yours to explore.

Lisbon's position just inland from the Atlantic helped it become the centre of a historic maritime empire that stretched from Brazil to Indonesia. The legacy is a flamboyant architecture typified by the Manueline structures of the riverside **Torre de Belém** and the magnificent **Mosteiro dos Jerónimos**. There's also an older, Moorish aspect to the warren of streets of the **Alfama** district, below the stunning hilltop **Castelo de São Jorge** and the medieval **Sé**. Lisbon's museums are equally diverse, from the historic works of art in the **Museu Nacional de Arte Antiga** to the panoply of international masterpieces in the **Museu Calouste Gulbenkian**.

Lisbon oozes history and tradition, but it is anything but staid. Nights out in the **Bairro Alto** or **Cais do Sodré** districts are memorable and there's a vibrancy to the city's street cafés and restaurants that's hard to match. Among the quaint old trams and cobbled streets, you'll also find some eye-catching modern architecture, typified by the futuristic **Parque das Nações**, which contains one of Europe's largest oceanariums.

Whether you're coming for a weekend or a week, our Top 10 guide brings together everything the city has to offer, from the coolest clubs to the best nearby beaches. There are tips throughout, from finding out what's free to choosing the best places to try local food specialities, plus eight easy-to-follow itineraries, designed to cover a range of sights in a short space of time. Add inspiring photography and detailed maps, and you've got the essential pocket-sized travel companion. **Enjoy the book, and enjoy Lisbon.**

Clockwise from top: *Neptune and Amphitrite in a Chariot*, Museu Nacional do Azulejo; tower at Quinta da Regaleira, Sintra; vaulted ceiling, Mosteiro dos Jerónimos; Torre de São Lourenço, Castelo de São Jorge; view from Castelo de São Jorge; Guincho beach; Portas do Sol viewpoint

Exploring Lisbon

It's great fun travelling around Lisbon, especially by tram or bus, which will take you to most of the city's historical buildings, parks and museums. Whether you're coming for a weekend, or want to get to know the city better, these two- and four-day itineraries will help you to make the most of your visit.

Mosteiros dos Jerónimos features an elaborate façade.

The views from the Castelo de São Jorge are some of Lisbon's finest.

Key
— Two-day itinerary
— Four-day itinerary

Two Days in Lisbon

Day ❶
MORNING
From the Baixa district, take the famous tram 28 to the **Sé Catedral** *(see pp16–17)*. After exploring its ancient interior, continue to the hilltop **Castelo de São Jorge** *(see pp12–13)*, a Moorish castle offering fantastic views over the city.
AFTERNOON
Head north to the **Museu Calouste Gulbenkian** *(see pp30–31)*. Housed in a modern cultural centre in attractive grounds, the museum displays an astonishing array of art – from ancient times to the 20th century.

Museu Nacional de Arte Antiga displays an exquisite collection of Portuguese art.

Day ❷
MORNING
Head west along the riverfront to the **Museu Nacional de Arte Antiga** *(see pp18–19)*. Set in a former palace, the museum contains paintings, furniture and other works of decorative art, much of it from Portugal's colonial days.
AFTERNOON
Travel west to the riverside suburb of Belém. Close to the stunning **Mosteiro dos Jerónimos** *(see pp14–15)* stands the **Torre de Belém** *(see pp22–3)*, built in the ornate Manueline style.

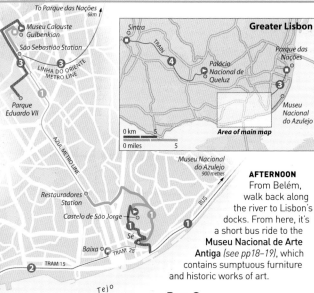

AFTERNOON
From Belém, walk back along the river to Lisbon's docks. From here, it's a short bus ride to the **Museu Nacional de Arte Antiga** (see pp18–19), which contains sumptuous furniture and historic works of art.

Four Days in Lisbon

Day ❶
MORNING
The best place to get an idea of Lisbon's layout is from the hilltop **Castelo de São Jorge** (see pp12–13). The ruined walls offer amazing views. From here, it's downhill to the **Sé Catedral** (see pp16–17), one of the city's oldest structures. Take time to explore the warren of streets below.

AFTERNOON
Take a bus east to the **Museu Nacional do Azulejo** (see pp26–7) to appreciate the amazing diversity of ceramic tiles (azulejos) that you'll see on many of the city's buildings. The museum is located inside the imposing Madre de Deus convent.

Day ❷
MORNING
Take tram 15 to the riverside suburb of Belém, packed with museums and monuments. Highlights include the **Mosteiro dos Jerónimos** (see pp14–15), and the nearby **Torre de Belém** (see pp22–3), built to defend the Tejo estuary.

Day ❸
MORNING
Take the metro to **Museu Calouste Gulbenkian** (see pp30–31), which houses an internationally acclaimed collection of artworks spanning 4,000 years of art history. Then head to the sloping Parque Eduardo VII for fine views over the city.

AFTERNOON
Travel northeast on the metro to the **Parque das Nações** (see pp20–21), a district built for Lisbon's Expo 98. It offers a cable car, a science museum, riverside walks and one of Europe's largest oceanariums.

Day ❹
MORNING
Take a train from the city to the **Palácio Nacional de Queluz** (see pp28–9), where the gardens and interiors show the lavish lifestyle enjoyed by the Portuguese royals.

AFTERNOON
Continue on the train to the village of **Sintra** (see pp32–3), a favoured summer hideaway for artists, monarchs and the wealthy. Much of it designated a UNESCO World Heritage Site, its highlights include the Palácio Nacional de Pena and Castelo dos Mouros.

Top 10 Lisbon Highlights

Interior at Palácio Nacional de Queluz

🔟 Lisbon Highlights

Lisbon is a city of immediate charms, and of a deeper beauty that must be sought out. One of the oldest cities in Europe, it is steeped in history, but not closed in on itself. Lisbon's youthful, modern side includes one of the liveliest and most diverse nightlife scenes in Europe.

1 Castelo de São Jorge
Crowning the hill where Lisbon's original settlers lived, this evocatively restored medieval castle boasts fabulous views *(see pp12–13)*.

Mosteiro dos Jerónimos 2
The Manueline is Portugal's own architectural style. Some of its greatest expressions can be seen in this glorious monastery *(see pp14–15)*.

3 The Sé
Lisbon's cathedral was built in the middle of the 12th century, just after the Christian reconquest. It is a fortress-like structure with stonework that glows amber as the sun sets *(see pp16–17)*.

4 Museu Nacional de Arte Antiga
Housed in a grand 17th-century palace, Portugal's national gallery displays a treasure trove of art, and places the country in historical context through its exhibits *(see pp18–19)*.

5 Parque das Nações
Flanked by the Vasco da Gama Bridge, the site of Lisbon's sea-themed Expo 98 has been transformed into a dynamic leisure, business and residential area *(see pp20–21)*.

⑥ Torre de Belém

The defensive tower at Belém is one of Lisbon's emblems, and one of the most perfectly proportioned examples of the Manueline style *(see pp22–3)*.

⑦ Museu Nacional do Azulejo

This museum is devoted to the quintessential Portuguese decorative element – the tile. It is also set in a stunning convent *(see pp26–7)*.

⑧ Palácio Nacional de Queluz

A Rococo feast, this summer palace just outside Lisbon was briefly the royal family's permanent residence. It exudes an air of ordered pleasure *(see pp28–9)*.

⑨ Museu Calouste Gulbenkian

A museum of international calibre, the Gulbenkian is a small and coolly pleasant universe of art history *(see pp30–31)*.

⑩ Sintra

Sintra is a powerful magnet, but it is wise to do as Lord Byron did, and absorb the city first before moving on to Sintra – the better to appreciate the contrast *(see pp32–3)*.

TOP 10 ⭐ Castelo de São Jorge

This hilltop castle is traditionally regarded as the site of Lisbon's founding settlement. Archaeological finds dated to the 7th century BC support this theory, although the oldest castle remains are from the Moorish era. Portugal's first king, Afonso Henriques, captured the Moorish citadel in 1147 and his successors added the Alcáçovas palace, which remained the royal residence until 1511. Following centuries of neglect, the castle was imaginatively restored in 1938, providing the city with one of its most attractive viewpoints.

1 Porta de São Jorge

This grand gate leads onto the final steep climb up to the castle grounds. In a wall niche to the left is a figure of St George. His local connection may derive from the role played by English troops in the conquest of Moorish Lisbon.

2 Casa do Leão

This restaurant, in one of Lisbon's most exclusive locations, serves traditional Portuguese and international food. Although the interior is very impressive (it was part of the 13th-century Alcáçovas palace), try to sit outside if you can – the views are superb.

The restored battlements at Castelo São Jorge

3 Castle Museum

On the site of the Alcáçovas palace, the museum (left) contains a collection of artifacts excavated from the hilltop, such as Iron Age cooking pots and 15th-century tiles.

4 Torre de Ulisses

In one of the inner battlement towers, a camera obscura attached to a periscope projects images of the city. The castle has a history of distant gazing: Lisbon's first observatory was set up there in 1779.

5 Torre de São Lourenço

Connected to the castle by a long series of steps **(left)**, this tower once formed part of the outer fortifications. Today, it offers another angle from which to view the castle.

6 Santa Cruz Neighbourhood

The tiny neighbourhood of Santa Cruz do Castelo, within the old citadel, is one of the most picturesque parts of Lisbon. It is home to ageing residents, younger investors and luxury hotels.

7 Inner Battlements

The reconstruction of the inner castle is one of the great achievements of the 1938 restoration. With ten towers and a dividing inner wall, the restored castle closely matches the layout and size of the original.

8 Archaeological Site

This site features traces of the most significant periods in Lisbon's history, including settlements from the Iron Age.

10 Esplanade

The esplanade **(above)** on top of the outer fortifications is one of the main rewards of a climb up to the castle. Dotted with archaeological remains and shaded by pines, it follows the castle's western perimeter, offering views of the river and lower city.

> **MYTHICAL MARTYR**
>
> The myth of Martim Moniz, a soldier who is said to have given his life as a doorstopper in 1147 – allowing Afonso Henriques and his crusaders to enter the castle – has a durable grip on the Lisbon imagination. The gate where his unverified deed took place bears his name, as does a square below the castle.

9 Statue of Afonso Henriques

This bronze statue of Portugal's first king **(right)** was added to the esplanade in 1947. It is a copy of an 1887 work by Soares dos Reis (the original is in Guimarães).

NEED TO KNOW

MAP G4 ▪ Porta de São Jorge, Rua de Santa Cruz do Castelo ▪ 218 800 620 ▪ www.castelodesaojorge.pt

Main castle complex: 9am–9pm (6pm Nov–Feb) daily

Torre de Ulisses camera obscura: 10am–5pm daily (depending on visibility)

Castle museum: 9am–9pm daily (6pm Nov–Feb). Adm: €8.50; concessions €5; family groups €20; under-10s free

▪ The west-facing esplanade is best in the late afternoon, when the sun is low.

▪ The outdoor bar at Chapitô (*see p66*) is a good place to relax after a visit to the castle.

TOP 10 ⭐ Mosteiro dos Jerónimos

Few of Lisbon's monuments are overly grand, and while this historic monastery is imposing, its proportions remain accessible. Begun in the 16th century by Diogo de Boytac and finished by João de Castilho and Jerónimo de Ruão, Jerónimos symbolizes Portugal's territorial expansion and expresses a uniquely national style. It's also a monument to Portuguese identity, housing tombs of men who helped make the country great, including navigator Vasco da Gama, Dom Sebastião and poet Luís de Camões.

1 South Portal
Restraint might not be the word for this towering sculpture of an entrance **(left)**, but look closely and you'll see that none of its parts is overpoweringly large. The figures include Henry the Navigator.

Nave 2
Many visitors find the well-lit nave **(right)** the most striking feature of Jerónimos, with its soaring carved pillars supporting a beautiful fan-vaulted ceiling.

NEED TO KNOW

MAP B6 ▪ Praça do Império, Belém ▪ 213 620 034 ▪ www.mosteiro jeronimos.pt

Open 10am–6:30pm (5:30pm Oct–Apr) Tue–Sun. Closed 1 Jan, Easter Sun, 1 May, 13 Jun, 25 Dec

Adm: €10; concessions €5; under-12s free; free on first Sun of month

▪ This is one of the most visited sites in Lisbon. Think twice before going at weekends, or mid-mornings or mid-afternoons (the latter two are favoured by tour groups). Hit it at lunchtime, or just before it closes, when the stone turns honey-coloured.

▪ After your visit, grab a bite to eat at nearby Cais de Belém *(see p89)*, and dine overlooking Jardim de Belém.

3 West Portal
The surrounds of this portal (now the main entrance) were sculpted by Nicolau Chanterène, and show the Manueline love of fantastical Renaissance decoration.

4 Cloister
The unique two-storey cloister is a lesson in Manueline tracery and lavish ornament **(above)**. It combines religious imagery, royal symbols and botanical motifs.

5 Refectory

The long, narrow refectory features fabulous vaulting and rope-like Manueline mouldings. The panel on the north wall (left) depicts the biblical story of the feeding of the 5,000.

STONE SURPRISES

Spend some time studying the carvings on the pillars in the nave and you will come across exotic plants and animals, along with exquisite human faces, and a few mythical figures. What better way to remind posterity that all this beauty was hewn by human hands, belonging to individuals who might occasionally let their imaginations roam free while carving.

8 Main Chapel

The current main chapel, dating from 1572, has a gridlike Mannerist layout. Look out for the tombs of Dom Manuel I and his wife Dona Maria (on the left) and Dom João III and his wife Dona Catarina (on the right).

9 Extension

Major restoration and extension works in the 19th century added the long, Neo-Manueline west wing, which now houses the Museu de Arqueologia and part of the Museu de Marinha (see p88). A distinctive domed bell tower was built to replace the previous pointed roof.

6 Tombs of Dom Sebastião and Cardinal D. Henrique

As you pass under the stellar vault of the crossing, look to each side to see the grand tombs of Cardinal D. Henrique and the young king Dom Sebastião.

7 Chapterhouse

Completed only in the 19th century, the attractive chapterhouse was never used as such. It houses the tomb of Alexandre Herculano, a celebrated 19th-century historian who also served as the first mayor of Belém.

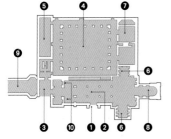

10 Tombs of Vasco da Gama and Luís de Camões

In the Lower Choir – facing the aisles under the gallery – are the tombs of Vasco da Gama (above) and Luís de Camões, transferred here in 1898.

TOP 10 ★ The Sé

Lisbon's cathedral was built shortly after Afonso Henriques had taken Lisbon from the Moors in 1147, and stands on a site once occupied by the city's main mosque. Today's crenellated Romanesque building is a much-restored reconstruction, rebuilt in various architectural styles following earthquake damage. It is also an archaeological site, with new finds made regularly beneath the cloister – originally excavated to reinforce the building's foundations.

4 Treasury
The first-floor Treasury is a museum of religious art, with some important holdings. It lost its greatest treasure, the relics of St Vincent (see p40), in the 1755 earthquake.

6 Cloister
The Gothic cloister, reached through one of the chapels, was an early addition to the cathedral. Some of its decoration anticipates the Manueline style – notice the varied patterns of the oculi.

1 Rose Window
Reconstructed using parts of the original, the rose window (above) softens the façade's rather severe aspect, but unfortunately lets in only a limited amount of light.

2 Bell Towers
These stocky towers – defining features of the Sé – recall those of Coimbra's earlier cathedral, built by the same master builder, Frei Roberto. A taller third tower collapsed during the 1755 earthquake (see p36).

3 St Anthony's Font
Tradition has it that Fernando Martins Bulhões (later St Anthony) was baptized in this font, which now features a tile panel of the saint preaching to the fishes. He is also said to have attended the cathedral school.

5 Gothic Ambulatory Chapels
The Chapel of São Cosme and São Damião is one of nine along the ambulatory. Look out for the tombs of nobleman Lopo Fernandes Pacheco (below) and his wife, Maria Villalobos.

FINDS FROM LISBON'S PAST

Archaeologically, the Sé is a work in progress – just like the castle (see pp12–13) and many other parts of central Lisbon. All this digging means that an increasing number of ancient remains are being uncovered. Public information can lag behind archaeological breakthroughs, but make a point of asking – you may be treated to a glimpse of the latest discovery.

7 Romanesque Nave

Little remains of the original cathedral beyond the renovated nave (above). It leads to a chancel enclosed by an ambulatory, a 14th-century addition.

9 13th-century Iron Railing

One of the ambulatory chapels is closed off by a 13th-century iron railing, the only one of its kind to survive in Portugal.

The distinctive bell towers of the Sé

8 Capela de Bartolomeu Joanes

This Gothic chapel, sponsored by a wealthy Lisbon merchant in 1324, contains the founder's tomb and a 15th-century Renaissance retable, painted by Cristóvão de Figueiredo, Garcia Fernandes and Diogo de Contreiras.

10 Archaeological Finds

Remains left by Moors, Visigoths, Romans and Phoenicians have been found in the excavation of the cloister (above).

NEED TO KNOW

MAP G4 ■ Largo de Sé
■ 218 866 752
Church: 9am–7pm daily
Cloister and Treasury:
10am–6:30pm Mon–Sat
Adm: €2.50; concessions €1.25

■ The Sé is a very dark church, and much of interest in the chapels is literally obscured. Head for the lighter cloister, and try to go in the afternoon, when the low light enters the façade's rose window.

■ A great place for a relaxed drink in the neighbourhood is the charming Pois, Café (see p66), where the Austrian owners are helping to keep Alfama cosmopolitan.

TOP 10 ⭐ Museu Nacional de Arte Antiga

Lisbon's Museu Nacional de Arte Antiga (MNAA) is Portugal's national gallery, a treasure trove of historically illuminating art. Housed in a 17th-century palace overlooking the river and port area, the museum was inaugurated in 1884. Today it contains a vast selection of European art dating from the 14th to the 19th centuries, and includes the most complete collection of Portuguese works in the world.

1 The Panels of St Vincent

A key Portuguese painting, this polyptych of around 1470 (probably by Nuno Gonçalves) portrays rich and poor in fascinating detail.

2 Martyrdom of St Sebastian

Painted by Gregório Lopes around 1536, this work was a part of a group of paintings intended to be placed on the altars of the Rotunda of the Convento de Cristo.

4 Portuguese and Chinese Ceramics

The museum's 7,500-piece collection of ceramics illustrates the interplay of international trade influences. From the 16th century, Portuguese faïence displays traces of Ming, while Chinese porcelain includes Portuguese coats of arms and other similar motifs.

5 Indo-Portuguese Furniture

The most interesting of the museum's furniture collections is probably the group of Indo-Portuguese pieces. The *contadores* **(left)** are many-drawered chests that combine orderliness with decorative abandon.

3 Chapel of St Albert

The chapel of the former Carmelite convent of Santo Alberto (currently closed for renovation) is decorated with *azulejos*.

NEED TO KNOW

MAP E5 ▪ Rua das Janelas Verdes ▪ 213 912 800 ▪ www.museudearteantiga.pt

Open 10am–6pm Tue–Sun. Closed 1 Jan, Easter Sun, 1 May, 13 Jun, 24 & 25 Dec

Adm: €6; concessions €3; under-12s free; free on first Sun of month

▪ There is a lot to see here, so study the layout and decide what to concentrate on. For 15 minutes with Nuno Gonçalves or Hieronymus Bosch, it may be worth giving the world's largest collection of 18th-century French silverware a miss.

▪ An alternative to the museum restaurant for lunch or dinner is the rooftop bar Le Chat (closed Mon in winter; www.lechat-lisboa.com).

6 Namban Screens

After encountering Portuguese travellers in the 16th century, Japan's artists portrayed them as *namban-jin*, or "southern barbarians". These screens **(below)** were never intended to be shown outside Japan.

8 St Jerome

This unusual portrait transcends the conventions of religious art. Painted in 1521 by Albrecht Dürer – who used a 93-year-old man from Antwerp as his model – it is above all a powerful portrayal of wisdom and old age.

LA NUIT DES MUSÉES

If you are in Lisbon in May, visit this museum at night to enjoy a programme of concerts and other events – not least the guided midnight tours. Part of a Europe-wide French initiative to make museum visits more than occasional Sunday afternoon outings, La Nuit des Musées gives access to the museum's treasures in a quite different context.

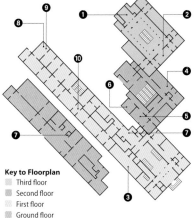

9 The Temptations of St Anthony

Hieronymus Bosch's three-panelled feast of fear and fantasy **(below)**, painted around 1500, is one of the museum's great treasures – and one of the world's great paintings.

Key to Floorplan

- Third floor
- Second floor
- First floor
- Ground floor

7 Garden, Restaurant and Shop

The museum's restaurant has lovely views of the garden and the river. There is a well-stocked gift shop on the first floor.

10 Conversation

Pieter de Hooch was a genre painter whose treatment of light was perhaps more complex than that of his contemporary, Vermeer. This work shows his key qualities as an artist.

🔟⭐ Parque das Nações

Built on the site of Lisbon's Expo 98 world exposition, held to mark the 500th anniversary of Vasco da Gama's epic voyage to India, the "Park of Nations" is a modern, self-contained riverside district east of the centre. It showcases contemporary Portuguese architecture, in stark contrast to the Manueline extravaganzas of historic Lisbon and Belém. A bustling amusement park and trade-fair centre by day, by night the park becomes a lively concert and events venue.

① Cable Car
Running most of the length of the Parque, the cable car **(above)** gives an overview of the area and views of the river and Vasco da Gama bridge. If the breeze is up, the cars may swing from side to side.

② Torre Vasco da Gama
At 145 m (476 ft), this is Lisbon's tallest building, albeit removed from the rest of the urban skyline. It is now part of a hotel and only guests have access to the viewing gallery.

③ Nautical Centre
The Doca dos Olivais nautical centre rents out equipment for various water sports and related activities.

④ Oceanário
The world's second-largest aquarium **(above)** has hundreds of aquatic species organized by habitat and viewed on two levels. The vast central tank has species large and small, but it's the cute sea otters in a side tank that get the most attention.

⑤ Restaurants
There are over 40 waterfront restaurants, many with outdoor seating. Popular for weekend lunches, they also form part of the Parque's nightlife scene.

⑥ Casino
A newer addition to the Parque, in the former Future Pavilion, the casino caters to all gamblers, offering slot machines, poker, roulette and blackjack.

7 Shops

Most shops **(left)** are in the Vasco da Gama centre, but there are also electronics and home interiors showrooms elsewhere in the Parque. Crowds flock to see the latest offers when the FIL trade-fair area puts on a consumer show.

CARD ADVANTAGES

The Lisboa Card ranges in price from €18.50 (valid for 24 hours) to €39 (72 hours). It provides free transport on the entire network (including the lifts and the train from Rossio to Sintra) and free entry to 25 places of interest. The card covers one adult, plus two children under the age of five. You can buy it online at www.askmelisboa.com.

NEED TO KNOW

MAP D1 ■ Avenida Dom João II ■ 218 919 898

Oceanário: 218 917 000
■ www.oceanario.pt
Open 10am–8pm daily (to 7pm in winter)
Adm: €14; concessions €9; under-4s free

Knowledge Pavilion – Ciência Viva: 218 917 100 ■ www.pavconhecimento.pt
Open 10am–6pm Tue–Fri, 11am–7pm Sat & Sun
Adm: €8; under-18s €6; over-65s €5; children 3–5 €4; under-3s free

Casino: www.casino-lisboa.pt

■ Summer afternoons here are hotter and more humid than in most of the city. The lawn next to the Oceanário and the riverfront benches are good spots for a rest.

8 Knowledge Pavilion – Ciência Viva

This large, child-friendly science museum is full of interactive multimedia exhibits, simulations, experiments and activities for various age groups, using cutting-edge technology.

9 Portugal Pavilion

With its concrete canopy suspended like a sail above the forecourt, the Portugal Pavilion **(below)** was once going to house the Council of Ministers. There are now plans to convert it into a museum and exhibition centre.

10 Gardens

Many of the rather anaemic-looking gardens planted for Expo 98 have grown into healthy patches of urban greenery, effectively softening the concrete and steel, particularly along the waterfront.

TOP 10 ⭐ Torre de Belém

The defensive tower at Belém is a jewel of the Manueline architectural style, combining Moorish, Renaissance and Gothic elements in a dazzling whole. It was built in 1514–20 by Francisco de Arruda, probably to a design by Diogo de Boytac. At that time, the tower stood on an island in the river Tejo, about 200 m (650 ft) from the northern bank, commanding the approach to Lisbon. The land between the tower and the Jerónimos monastery has since been reclaimed.

1 Battlements
The merlons of most of the tower's battlements are decorated with the cross of the Order of Christ, carved to look like features on a shield. The smaller merlons at the rear and on top of the tower are crowned with pyramid-shaped spikes.

2 Watchtowers
You can't miss the Moorish-influenced watchtowers **(below)**. Their domes are seated on Manueline rope-like circles and rise to a pile of small spheres reminiscent of the tops of chess pieces.

Dazzling carved exterior of the Torre de Belém

4 Virgin and Child Sculpture
A statue of Our Lady of Safe Homecoming stands by the light well that was used to lower cannons into the dungeon. She evokes the intrepid explorers of Portugal's past, but also everyday sailors – and the concerned longing for absent husbands and sons known in Portugal as *saudade*.

3 Exhibitions
The tower's former dungeon, now quite bright, is often used for temporary exhibitions, as well as for a permanent information display for visitors and a gift shop.

5 Governor's Room
Now empty, this room was used by the tower's first governor, Gaspar de Paiva. After it became obsolete, lighthouse keepers and customs officials worked here. The room's acoustics amplify even the slightest whisper.

6 Rhinoceros Detail
Each of the sentry boxes is supported by a naturalistically carved stone. The rhinoceros on the northwestern box is the most famous, thought to be the first European carving of this animal. Time has now rounded its features.

7 Renaissance Loggia

An arcaded loggia overlooks the main deck – comparisons to a ship are unavoidable here. The loggia breaks with the military style of most of the building and adds a theatrical element, while the railing and tracery of the balustrade **(left)** are pure Manueline. Balconies on each side of the tower echo the loggia's style.

8 Manueline Twists

Ropes and knots were the main theme for the Manueline masons here. The tracery of some of the balustrades features the near-organic shapes that would be developed in later Manueline buildings.

9 Dungeon

From the tower's vaulted bottom level **(below)** – also used as a dungeon – 17 cannon once covered the approaches to Lisbon.

10 Armillary Spheres

The armillary spheres carved above the loggia were instruments for showing the motion of the stars around the earth. They became a symbol of Portugal, and still feature on the national flag.

HOLY NAMESAKE

Belém means Bethlehem – and the name is taken from a chapel dedicated to St Mary of Bethlehem, built in the mid-15th century near the river's edge, in what was then Restelo. This chapel subsequently gave way to the grand Jerónimos church and monastery; the church is still known as Santa Maria de Belém. The name Restelo, for its part, now applies to the area above and behind Belém, a leafy district of fine residences and embassy buildings.

NEED TO KNOW

MAP A6 ■ Avda Brasília
■ 213 620 034 ■ www. torrebelem.pt

Open 10am–5:30pm Tue–Sun (last adm 5pm; to 6:30pm May–Sep). Closed 1 Jan, Easter Sun, 1 May, 13 Jun, 25 Dec

Adm: €6; senior citizens €3; Youth Card holders €3; under-12s free; free first Sun of month

■ The tower is at its prettiest in the early morning or late afternoon. Tour groups tend to visit early, so go as late as you can for a quieter visit.

■ Nearby restaurants (including Vela Latina – *see p89)* often fill up quickly; if you can't find a table, cross the railway line by the footbridge and walk to the nearby Centro Cultural de Belém. Este Oeste, the restaurant here, has great food and a terrace.

Following pages The cloister of the Sé

🔟 ⭐ Museu Nacional do Azulejo

Ceramic tiles, or *azulejos*, are a distinctive aspect of Portuguese culture, featuring in contexts both mundane and sacred. The art of making them is a Moorish inheritance, much adapted – most noticeably in the addition of human figures, which Islam forbids. This museum dedicated to tiles is enjoyable both for the excellent displays and for its beautiful setting, a 16th-century convent transformed over the centuries to include some of the city's prettiest cloisters and one of its most richly decorated churches.

Lisbon Panel ①

This vast tiled panorama of Lisbon **(right)**, 23 m (75 ft) in length, is a captivating depiction of the city's waterfront as it looked in about 1740, before the great earthquake. It was transferred here from one of the city's palaces.

② Manueline Cloister

This small but stunning cloister **(above)** is one of the few surviving features of the original convent of Madre de Deus. This is the Manueline style at its most restrained. The geometrical wall tiles were added in the 19th century.

③ Nossa Senhora da Vida Altarpiece

Almost 5 m (16 ft) square and containing over 1,000 tiles, this 16th-century Renaissance altarpiece is the work of Marçal de Matos. It depicts the *Adoration of the Shepherds*, flanked by St Luke and St John.

④ Tile-Making Exhibit

Step-by-step exhibits on tile-making, from a lump of clay to final glazing, illuminate how the medium combines the practical and decorative.

⑤ Renaissance Cloister

Part of the first major alteration to the convent in the 16th century, this airy, two-level cloister is the work of Diogo de Torralva. Glassed in to protect visitors and the collection from the weather, it is the light heart of the building.

⑥ Temporary Exhibitions

The ground and first floors have temporary exhibitions on subjects like contemporary tile art, an important art form in Portugal.

7 Moorish Tiles
With their attractive geometric patterns, varied colour palettes and glazing techniques, Moorish tiles **(left)** continue to inspire tile-makers and home decorators alike.

8 Shop
Numerous quality reproductions of classic tile designs are available, as well as modern tiles and other gifts.

Key to Floorplan
- Second floor
- First floor
- Ground floor

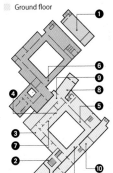

A NOD FROM THE 19TH CENTURY
When the southern façade of the church was restored in the late 19th century, the architect used as his model a painting now in the Museu de Arte Antiga (see pp18–19). This shows the convent and church as they looked in the early 16th century. Indoors, the quest for authenticity was less zealous. In one of the cloisters, 19th-century restorers have left a potent symbol of their own era: an image of a steam locomotive has been incorporated into one of the upper-level capitals.

9 Cafeteria and Winter Garden
Suitably tiled with food-related motifs, the museum cafeteria is worth a stop for coffee or a light lunch. The courtyard is partly covered and forms a winter garden.

NEED TO KNOW
MAP C2 ▪ Rua da Madre de Deus 4 ▪ 218 100 340 ▪ www.museu doazulejo.pt

Open 10am–6pm Tue–Sun. Closed 1 Jan, Easter Sun, 1 May, 13 Jun, 25 Dec

Adm: €5; senior citizens €2.50; Youth Card holders €2.50; under-12s free; free on first Sun of month

▪ The rather awkward location of the Tile Museum can be turned into an asset if you combine it with a visit to Parque das Nações (see pp20–21), a shopping trip to Santa Apolónia (see p55), or lunch at D'Avis (see p67).

▪ The best place for a drink is the museum's cafeteria; otherwise, head for Santa Apolónia (see p55).

10 Madre de Deus Church
The magnificent barrel-vaulted convent church **(above)**, packed with paintings, is the result of three centuries of construction and decoration. Its layout dates from the 16th century; the tile panels and gilt woodwork are 17th- and 18th-century.

TOP 10 ⭐ Palácio Nacional de Queluz

Queluz is like a miniature Versailles – an exquisite Rococo palace with formal gardens and parkland, just 15 minutes from central Lisbon. Prince Pedro, younger son of Dom João V, had it built as a summer palace in 1747–52. Thirteen years later, when he married his niece, the future Dona Maria I, he commissioned extensions from the French architect Jean-Baptiste Robillon, in order to make it the permanent royal residence. Queluz had a brief golden era before the royal family fled to Brazil after Napoleon's invasion in 1807.

2 Gardens

A pair of formal gardens – the Neptune Garden **(above)** and Malta Garden – occupy the space between the palace's two asymmetric wings. Laid out by Robillon, they are adorned with fountains, statues and topiary.

3 Sala dos Embaixadores

The magnificent Ambassadors' Room was used for diplomatic audiences, and is opulently decorated with stuccowork and painted and gilded carved woodwork. Concerts were also held in these grand surroundings and the *trompe l'oeil* ceiling depicts the royal family at such an event.

1 Robillon Pavilion

This impressive building **(above)**, replete with windows, balustrades and pillars, is a bit too fussy for purists. It was designed by the French architect Robillon.

NEED TO KNOW

MAP A2 ■ Largo do Palácio ■ 219 237 300 ■ www.parquesde sintra.pt

Open 9am–7pm daily (5:30pm in winter); reduced ticket available after 3:30pm. Closed 1 Jan, 25 Dec

Adm: €10; senior citizens €8.50; children 6–17 €8.50; under-6s free; gardens only €5

■ An early-morning visit to Queluz can be combined with a trip to Sintra (see pp32–3).

■ The terrace at the Pousada is the best place for a drink – unless you are lucky enough to have an invitation to an event in the palace itself.

7 Corredor das Mangas

The hallway linking the old and newer parts of Queluz was named for the glass sleeves (*mangas*) of its candles. Painted wall tiles **(left)** give it its other name, the *Corredor dos Azulejos*.

4 Throne Room

Competing in grandeur with the Sala dos Embaixadores, the dome-ceilinged Throne Room also served as the palace's ballroom, church and theatre.

THE WAILING QUEEN

Dona Maria I, after she became queen and then lost a son, famously lost her mind. Visitors described hearing her wailing as she wandered the corridors of Queluz. She was exiled to Brazil in 1807 with her younger son, then Regent, to escape the humiliating invasion of Portugal led by the French Emperor Napoleon.

8 Cozinha Velha and Pousada Dona Maria I

The old palace kitchens have long housed the fine Cozinha Velha restaurant. A drink on the terrace of the newer Pousada Dona Maria I, in the former quarters of the Royal Guard, is as close as you'll get to living at Queluz.

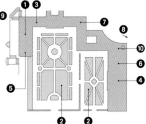

9 Lion Staircase

This beautiful staircase links the lower parkland to the palace. It is flanked by an arcaded "dwarf gallery" with a cascade flowing into a tiled canal; the royal family went boating here.

10 Chapel

The first room to be completed in 1752, the chapel also held concerts, some by Dona Maria I's own chamber orchestra. It is thought that she and her sisters painted some of the wall panels.

5 Don Quixote Chamber

The inlaid circular-pattern floor and domed ceiling make this square room seem round. It is named for its painted scenes from *Don Quixote*.

6 Music Room

The Music Room **(right)** was used for concerts and even opera performances, and doubled as a venue for important christenings. It still serves as a concert venue.

🔟 ⭐ Museu Calouste Gulbenkian

Based on the private collections of oil millionaire Calouste Gulbenkian, this museum spans over 4,000 years of art history while remaining manageable for the visitor. Internationally recognized for its quality, the museum is part of a complex that houses the headquarters of the Calouste Gulbenkian Foundation, a concert hall and auditoria for its orchestra and choir, an art library, a peaceful park and a modern art museum.

1 3rd Dynasty Egyptian Bowl

Found in a tomb north of Thebes, this elegant alabaster bowl was modelled on an everyday ointment bowl. The ancient Egyptians adorned tombs with copies of everyday objects made from noble materials. This one is 4,000 years old.

2 Ancient Greek Vase

This 5th-century BC wide-rimmed terracotta vase **(right)** is decorated with mythological motifs: the abduction of Phoebe and Hilaira by Castor and Pollux, and a bacchanalian scene.

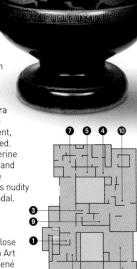

4 Diana Statue

A graceful marble statue by the French sculptor Jean-Antoine Houdon, dating from 1780, is unusual for the era in that it depicts the goddess in movement, and completely naked. It belonged to Catherine the Great of Russia and was exhibited at the Hermitage, where its nudity caused quite a scandal.

3 St Catherine and St Joseph

Two paintings by the 15th-century Flemish master Rogier van der Weyden are believed to be parts of an altarpiece; a third element is in London's National Gallery. The female **(above)** is thought to be Catherine of Alexandria.

5 Lalique Collection

Gulbenkian was a close friend of the French Art Nouveau jeweller René Lalique and bought a great number of his graceful pieces, many on show in this part of the museum.

6 Oriental Islamic Art

This large gallery displays a wide-ranging collection of manuscripts, carpets, textiles, ceramics **(above)** and other objects from Turkey, Syria, the Caucasus (including Armenia), Persia and India.

7 Boy Blowing Bubbles

Édouard Manet's 1867 painting **(right)** is not just a version of the popular allegory on the transience of life and art, but a deftly painted portrait of Léon-Édouard Koëlla, stepson of the artist.

8 Yuan Dynasty Stem Cup

This blue-glazed piece, dating from an earlier period (1279–1368) than most of the Far Eastern collection, is decorated with delicate reliefs of Taoist figures under bamboo leaves.

THE SPOILS OF OIL

Calouste Sarkis Gulbenkian was an Armenian who made his huge fortune by negotiating the transfer of assets between oil companies – each time earning a five per cent commission. He came to Lisbon during World War II, staying at the Hotel Aviz until his death in 1955. His will stipulated that a foundation be set up in Portugal to look after his vast collection and to support the arts.

9 Portrait of an Old Man

This engaging *chiaroscuro* portrait of a bearded man is an example of Rembrandt's preoccupation with ageing. The gaze is tired, and the large hands intricately lined. Nothing is known about the model.

NEED TO KNOW

MAP F1 ■ Avenida de Berna 45A ■ 217 823 000 ■ www.museu.gulbenkian.pt

Open 10am–6pm Wed–Mon. Closed 1 Jan, Easter Sun, 1 May, 25 Dec

Adm: €5; students and over-65s €2.50; under-12s free; free on Sun

....

■ The Centro de Arte Moderna José Azeredo Perdigão – also part of the Gulbenkian Foundation – has a good collection of contemporary Portuguese art, and stages frequent temporary shows.

■ There are good cafés at both museums.

10 Louis XV and XVI Furniture

Considered ostentatious by some, the 18th-century French pieces **(above)** in the decorative art collection fascinate for their materials and craftsmanship. Highlights include a Louis XV chest inlaid with lacquer panels, gold leaf, mother-of-pearl, bronze and ebony; and a table with a shelf that flips over to reveal a mirror.

🔟 ⭐ Sintra

Recognized in 1995 as a UNESCO World Heritage Site, Sintra was the summer residence for Portuguese kings from the 13th to the late 19th centuries. It still possesses many of the classic qualities of a hill retreat: a cooler climate than the city, ample greenery and an atmosphere conducive to romantic whims. The old town is pretty but crowded, while the surrounding landscapes and sights are an essential part of any visit.

Quinta da Regaleira ③

This lavish palace **(right)** looms on a steep bend in the old road to Sintra. It was built around 1900 for António Augusto Carvalho Monteiro, an eccentric millionaire who also owned Peninha *(see p104)*. He was a bibliophile and keen dabbler in alchemy and other esoteric subjects.

① Monserrate

A fantastic Moorish-style palace **(above)** dominates the gardens of Monserrate, which were laid out by English residents.

④ São Pedro Market

Antiques are a feature of the lively market held in the suburb of São Pedro on the second and fourth Sundays of each month.

⑥ Palácio de Seteais

Built in 1787, Seteais (now a hotel) got its Neo-Classical façade later. It's best to visit well dressed, for tea or a meal.

② Palácio Nacional da Pena

Dom Fernando II, Dona Maria II's German-born king consort, had this fabulous toyland palace built in the mid-19th century. The work of a lively imagination, it exhibits his eclectic tastes, and is preserved as it was when the royal family lived there **(above)**.

⑤ Parque da Pena

Filled with exotic trees and shrubs, the park around the Palácio da Pena is another of Dom Fernando II's contributions to Sintra's magic. It contains the chalet he had built for his second wife, Elise Hensler, an American opera singer.

⑨ Palácio Nacional de Sintra

Twin conical chimneys mark the former royal palace **(left)**. Begun in the 14th century and extended in the 16th, it is a captivating mix of styles from Moorish to Renaissance.

THE ARTIST KING

Ferdinand Saxe-Coburg-Gotha was known in Portugal as Dom Fernando II, the "artist" king. Like his cousin Prince Albert, who married the English Queen Victoria, he loved art, nature and the new inventions of the time. He was himself a watercolour painter. Ferdinand enthusiastically adopted his new country and devoted his life to patronizing the arts. His lifelong dream of building the extravagant Palace of Pena was achieved in 1885, although his death meant that he didn't see its completion.

⑩ Centro Cultural Olga Cadaval

Sintra's main cultural venue, a modern centre hosting dance, theatre, concerts and films, was built in 1987, after a fire destroyed much of the Carlos Manuel cinema.

⑦ Parque da Liberdade

The town park, with its steep paths running among the trees, occupies the valley below the old town.

Castelo dos Mouros ⑧

This 10th-century castle **(right)** was captured by Afonso Henriques in 1147. Dom Fernando II partially rebuilt it in the 19th century. A chapel, with an exhibition about the castle's history, and a Moorish cistern are inside.

NEED TO KNOW

▪ Tourist information: Praça da República 23, Sintra; 219 231 157; www.cm-sintra.pt, www.parquesdesintra.pt

▪ Sintra lies 30 km (18 miles) northwest of Lisbon. Trains run from Lisbon's Rossio and Entrecampos stations.

▪ Sintra's romantic and refreshing qualities may be seriously challenged on summer weekends, when tour groups and locals collide in the square in front of the Palácio Nacional de Sintra. Go during the week, and avoid midday in summer.

▪ Bars and cafés in the old town fill up quickly and charge inflated prices. For a different atmosphere, walk past the Tourist Office to Lawrence's Hotel *(see p116)* and enjoy a refreshment in one of its small, cozy, colonial-style public rooms.

The Top 10 of Everything

View from the Torre de Belém

🔟 Moments in History

① 138 BC: Roman Occupation

Despite reaching the Iberian peninsula in the second century BC, it took the Romans almost a century to conquer its westernmost parts. The trading post of Olisipo (Lisbon's Greek name) was occupied in 138 BC.

② 714: Moorish Occupation
Roman Lisbon was invaded by Alan tribes from the north, about whom little is known, and then by the Visigoths, who ruled from Toledo. The Visigoths were swept from power by Moorish armies crossing into Iberia at the Straits of Gibraltar. Lisbon fell to the Moors in 714.

③ 1147: Reconquest
The Christian reconquest began in the north, where Afonso Henriques founded the Portuguese kingdom – as distinct from the future Spanish kingdom of León – in 1140. His armies took Lisbon following a three-month siege in 1147.

④ 1497: Vasco da Gama Sails from Belém

The high point of Portugal's era of discovery was Vasco da Gama's voyage to India. Rounding the Cape of Good Hope, he proved Columbus wrong and gave the Portuguese the competitive edge in the spice trade.

Afonso Henriques captures Lisbon

⑤ 1640: Independence from Spain

Spain had usurped the Portuguese throne in 1581, after the death of Dom Sebastião and many of the Portuguese nobility in a north African military adventure. The 1640 coup at Lisbon's royal palace reinstated self-rule and proclaimed the Duke of Bragança king of Portugal.

⑥ 1755: The Great Earthquake

On 1 November 1755, a massive earthquake struck southern Portugal and laid waste to central Lisbon. Three shocks were followed by devastating fires and tidal waves.

An earthquake wrecks Lisbon, 1755

1910: Portugal Becomes a Republic

In 1908, Dom Carlos and his heir were assassinated by republican activists in Terreiro do Paço. The king's surviving son became Dom Manuel II, but abdicated in October 1910 in the face of a republican revolution. The Republic was formalized on 5 October.

8 1933: The New State

António de Oliveira Salazar, who had been appointed finance minister in the hope that he could solve the country's financial crisis, was asked to form a government in 1932. The following year his new constitution was passed by parliament, in effect making him an authoritarian dictator.

The Carnation Revolution

1974: The Carnation Revolution

Salazar's successor Marcelo Caetano and his government were overthrown by a group of army captains on 25 April. Three men were killed by shots from the headquarters of the PIDE, the political police, as crowds cheered the end of its reign of fear.

1986: European Union Membership

After a few tumultuous years following the 1974 revolution, a stable democracy was established in Portugal. EU membership brought a boost to the economy through both subsidies and foreign investment. In 2007, the Lisbon Treaty was signed in Belém. Portugal was badly hit by the global economic crisis, however, and austerity continues to this day.

TOP 10 HISTORICAL FIGURES

António de Oliveira Salazar

1 Viriato
Legendary leader of the Lusitanians, a Celtic-Iberian tribe that resisted Roman occupation for two decades.

2 Tariq
As Berber leader of the Moorish force, Tariq conquered most of the Iberian peninsula in 711–16.

3 Afonso Henriques
Having taken control of the countship of Portucale, Afonso was calling himself "Portucalense king" by 1140.

4 Henry the Navigator
Son of Dom João, Prince Henry was the architect of Portugal's early overseas expansion in the 15th century.

5 Duke of Bragança
Although hesitant at first, the duke agreed to be king, becoming Dom João IV after the 1640 coup.

6 Marquis of Pombal
Chief minister under Dom José I, Pombal reconstructed the city after the earthquake of 1755, but was later reviled as a despot by Dona Maria I.

7 Eça de Queiroz
The 19th-century chronicler of Lisbon was a member of the Cenáculo, a group of writers who were opposed to the monarchy.

8 António de Oliveira Salazar
Portugal's deceptively low-key dictator was formerly a professor of economics.

9 Mário Soares
The first democratically elected post-revolution prime minister won a second term and, in 1986, became president of Portugal.

10 Aníbal Cavaco Silva
Leader of the Social Democrats and prime minister from 1985 to 1995, he was elected president in 2006 and again in 2011.

🔟 Museums and Galleries

Central panels from *The Panels of St Vincent* (1460s), Nuno Gonçalves

① Museu Nacional de Arte Antiga

Portugal's national museum houses priceless national and international works, including painting, sculpture, textiles and decorative art. It is sometimes called the Museu das Janelas Verdes due to the building's location in Rua das Janelas Verdes as well as its green windows *(see pp18–19)*.

② Museu Nacional do Azulejo

Housed in a stunning convent and church, Lisbon's popular *azulejo* museum covers tiles and tile-making comprehensively, and has a pleasant café-restaurant *(see pp26–7)*.

③ Museu do Design e da Moda (MUDE)

MAP M5 ▪ Rua Augusta 24 ▪ 218 886 117 ▪ 10am–6pm Tue–Sun ▪ www.mude.pt

MUDE showcases 20th-century design from around the world.

Star exhibits include Eames chairs and dresses from Dior's landmark 1947 New Look collection *(see p56)*.

④ Museu Calouste Gulbenkian

The Armenian oil baron and art collector Calouste Gulbenkian could well be the most important person in Portuguese postwar cultural life. His museum is a rare treat, not just because it covers so much in such a manageable way, but also because it has pleasant gardens and a good contemporary arts centre on site *(see pp30–31)*.

⑤ Galeria 111

MAP C2 ▪ Campo Grande 113A ▪ 217 977 418 ▪ 10am–7pm Tue–Sat

Since opening in 1964, this uptown contemporary art gallery has exhibited artists such as Paula Rego, Júlio Pomar and Joana Vasconcelos.

⑥ Museu Nacional dos Coches

MAP B6 ▪ Praça Afonso de Albuquerque ▪ 210 732 319 ▪ 10am–6pm Tue–Sun ▪ Adm ▪ www.museudoscoches.pt

A coach museum is the sort of place you might not visit if you didn't have a special interest in the subject. But this is one of Lisbon's most popular museums, thanks to its collection of 68 horse-drawn coaches and the connections they create with the past *(see p88)*.

Exhibit at the Museu Nacional dos Coches

7 Zé dos Bois
MAP K4 ▪ Rua da Barroca 59
▪ 213 430 205 ▪ 3–11pm Wed–Sat
▪ Adm ▪ www.zedosbois.org

ZDB, as it is also known, has consistently been Lisbon's most inspirational and genuinely "alternative" gallery. It is also a Bairro Alto bar.

8 Museu Nacional de Arte Contemporânea do Chiado (MNAC)

Guardian of Portuguese modernity in art, this museum *(see p78)* has a collection extending from the mid-19th century to the 21st century, though the decades after 1950 are less fully covered. There are also temporary exhibitions and an enjoyable courtyard café-restaurant.

Gallery in the MNAC

9 Lisbon Story Centre
MAP N5 ▪ Praça do Comércio 78–81 ▪ 211 941 099 ▪ 10am–8pm daily ▪ Adm ▪ www.lisboastory centre.pt

This museum offers a romp through Lisbon's history, presented in a series of rooms. Each period of time is recreated through models, paintings and multimedia displays, including a 4D version of the 1755 earthquake.

10 Fundação/Museu Arpad Szenes-Vieira da Silva
MAP F3 ▪ Praça das Amoreiras 56–8
▪ 213 880 044 ▪ 10am–6pm Tue–Sun
▪ Adm (free first Sun of month)
▪ www.fasvs.pt

This museum is devoted to the work of Portuguese modernist Maria Helena Vieira da Silva and her Hungarian husband, Arpad Szenes.

TOP 10 PORTUGUESE ARTISTS

1 Nuno Gonçalves
Nuno is believed to be the 15th-century painter of *The Panels of St Vincent*, which may contain his self-portrait.

2 Grão Vasco (Vasco Fernandes)
One of Portugal's best-known 16th-century painters (c.1475–1542) is known for his Flemish-style altarpieces.

3 Josefa de Óbidos
The work of this female painter and engraver (1630–84) falls between the Mannerist and the Baroque styles.

4 Joaquim Machado de Castro
This celebrated sculptor (1731–1822) is best known for his equestrian statue of Dom José I in Praça do Comércio.

5 José Malhoa
A naturalistic painter (1855–1933) most famous for creating the deliciously languorous *O Fado*.

6 Columbano Bordalo Pinheiro
A gifted portraitist, Columbano (1857–1929) painted many of the leading figures of the Republican movement.

7 Júlio Pomar
One of Portugal's most important 20th-century painters, Pomar (b.1926) was at odds with the Fascist dictatorship.

8 Paula Rego
Portugal-born Rego (b.1935) is best known for producing haunting prints and paintings based on children's books and Portuguese folk stories.

9 João Cutileiro
Portugal's best-known living sculptor (b.1937) is renowned for his marble works depicting women's torsos.

10 Joana Vasconcelos
Feminist artist Vasconcelos (b.1971) subverts mundane objects, taking them out of their everyday context and transforming them into sculptures.

***O Fado* (1910), José Malhoa**

🔟 Churches and Monasteries

1 Mosteiro dos Jerónimos
The country's most significant monument displays the exuberant, almost oriental ornamentation that is a chief characteristic of the Manueline style *(see pp14–15)*.

2 The Sé
Seen at a distance, Lisbon's cathedral can almost conjure up the mosque that preceded it. Up close, the Romanesque building is attractively simple *(see pp16–17)*.

3 Igreja de São Domingos
MAP M3 ■ Largo de São Domingos ■ 7:30am–7pm daily
One of Lisbon's oldest churches is one of its hardiest survivors. Built in 1242, it was damaged in the earthquakes of 1531 and 1755, and ravaged by fire in 1959. The blackened interior brings to mind the days when Inquisition processions would end with charred corpses.

4 Basílica da Estrela
MAP E4 ■ Praça da Estrela ■ 7:45am–1pm & 4–8pm Mon, 7:45am–1pm & 3–8pm Tue–Fri, 9:30am–1pm & 3–8pm Sat, 8am–1pm & 3–8pm Sun (mass at 9am)
This domed landmark was built from 1779 to give thanks for the birth of a male heir to Dona Maria I. Sadly, the boy died of smallpox before the church was finished. Inside is the queen's tomb, and a nativity scene with over 500 cork-and-terracotta figures; ask the sacristan to show it to you.

The Baroque Panteão Nacional

5 Panteão Nacional
MAP R3 ■ Campo de Santa Clara ■ 10am–5pm Tue–Sun (Apr–Oct: 10am–6pm) ■ Adm
An unmistakable feature of the city's eastern skyline, this Baroque beauty is famous for having taken 284 years to build. Otherwise known as Igreja de Santa Engrácia, the National Pantheon houses cenotaphs to national heroes, hence the groups of schoolchildren clustered around inside.

6 São Vicente de Fora
MAP Q3 ■ Largo de São Vicente 3 ■ Church: 9am–1pm, 2:30–5pm Tue–Sun; Monastery: 10am–5pm Tue–Sun ■ Adm (monastery)
In 1173, when St Vincent was proclaimed patron saint of Portugal, his relics were moved from the Algarve to the original church on this site. Philip II of Spain had the present Mannerist church built in the early 1600s. In 1885 the refectory was turned into the pantheon of the Bragança royal family.

7 Igreja de Santo António
MAP N4 ■ Largo de Santo António à Sé ■ 8am–7pm Mon–Fri (8pm Sat & Sun)
Lisbon's patron saint was allegedly born here (as Fernando Bulhões) in the late 12th century. The present Baroque church replaced the one lost to the 1755 earthquake. Weddings are held here in June – it's thought that St Anthony brings luck to newlyweds.

Interior of the Basílica da Estrela

8 Igreja de São Roque

MAP K3 ■ Largo Trindade Coelho ■ Apr–Sep: 2–7pm Mon, 9am–7pm Tue, Wed & Fri–Sun, 9am–8pm Thu; Oct–Mar: 2–6pm Mon, 9am–6pm Tue–Sun

Built in the 16th century for the Jesuit order, this church is famous for its opulent interior, particularly the Chapel of St John the Baptist. Created in Rome using lapis lazuli, agate, alabaster, amethyst, precious marbles, gold and silver, it was blessed by the pope, taken apart and sent to Lisbon in three ships.

9 Igreja do Carmo

MAP L4 ■ Largo do Carmo ■ 10am–7pm Mon–Sat (Oct–May: 10am–6pm) ■ Adm

The late 14th-century church and convent of Carmo was one of Lisbon's main places of worship before the roof caved in on All Saints' Day 1755, killing the congregation. The evocative ruin, with its bare Gothic arches, now houses an archaeological museum.

Ruined arches of Igreja do Carmo

10 Igreja da Graça

MAP P2 ■ Largo da Graça ■ 9am–5pm Tue–Fri, 9am–6pm Sat, 10am–1pm & 5–8pm Sun

This 1271 Augustinian monastery, rebuilt after the 1755 earthquake, is home to the Senhor dos Passos, a figure of Christ bearing the cross.

TOP 10 MANUELINE GEMS

Jerónimos Cloister

1 Torre de Belém
More decorative than defensive today, this tower is a perfect example of the Manueline style.

2 Jerónimos Cloister
João de Castilho's cloister boasts the entire arsenal of Manueline features. Take your time here.

3 South Portal of Jerónimos
This riot of decoration – featuring saints, royals and other symbols – is actually completely symmetrical.

4 Nave of Jerónimos
Mixing organic elements with geometry, octagonal piers encrusted with carvings rise up to the web-like vaulting.

5 Conceição Velha Portal
This Manueline portal is the only remnant of the original 16th-century church, which was destroyed in the 1755 earthquake.

6 Portal, Museu do Azulejo
This dates from the 19th century, when the façade was reconstructed from a 16th-century painting.

7 Manueline Cloister, Museu do Azulejo
This small and relatively restrained cloister is a reminder of the building's 16th-century role as a convent.

8 Ermida de São Jerónimo
This simple chapel from 1514 gives the Manueline a broader, more contemporary aesthetic.

9 Casa dos Bicos
This 16-century private palace combines Italian-style architecture with Manueline windows.

10 Rossio Station
A nostalgic Neo-Manueline look back from 1892, with a hint of parallels to Art Nouveau.

🔟 City Views

Magnificent view over the Baixa and the Tejo from Santa Luzia

1 Santa Luzia
MAP P4

This romantic viewpoint by the church of Santa Luzia has a pergola with tiled pillars, walls and benches. The veranda has dazzling vistas over the Alfama and across the river, a view shared by the adjacent café.

2 Castelo de São Jorge
MAP N3

The view from under the umbrella pines on the castle's esplanade takes in Alfama, the Baixa, Bairro Alto on the hill opposite, and the river. The light here is particularly appealing in the late afternoon. It is also a great spot from which to watch the sun set.

3 São Pedro de Alcântara
MAP K2

This small garden is one of Lisbon's best-known viewpoints. Bougainvillea tumbles onto the next terrace, a more formal and less accessible garden. The view extends across Restauradores and the Baixa to the Sé and the castle.

4 Miradouro de Santa Catarina
MAP J5

Not just a visual vantage point, this is also a place to meet and hang out. A sculpture of Adamastor, the mythical creature from Camões' epic poem *The Lusiads*, presides over events from a stone plinth. There's a wide view of the river, encompassing the station at Cais do Sodré, the Alcântara docks and the 25 de Abril bridge.

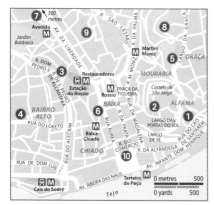

5 Igreja da Graça
MAP P2

The pine-shaded esplanade by the Graça church has a café with a classic view of the lower city, the river and the bridge. Like the castle's viewpoint, this one is best visited in the late afternoon.

6 Elevador de Santa Justa

The best close-up overview of the Baixa and Rossio, with the castle looming above, is to be had from the terrace at the top of the Elevador de Santa Justa *(see p70)*. It is reached via an extremely tight spiral staircase, but the view is definitely worth the climb.

7 Parque Eduardo VII
MAP F2

Many visitors find it difficult to feel any real affection for Eduardo VII park, with its formal plan, its football-killing slope and its lack of shade. But climb to the top and the architect's plan makes sense, as Lisbon stretches away from you in an unbroken perspective right down to the river. The sides of the park have a less commanding view but offer more shade and human interest.

Panorama from Senhora do Monte

8 Senhora do Monte
MAP P1

One of the highest vantage points in the city, Our Lady of the Mount (there is a small chapel behind the viewpoint) affords a grand vista that encompasses the castle, the Graça church and the Mouraria quarter, as well as the Tejo estuary, the lower city, midtown Lisbon and the Monsanto park.

9 Jardim do Torel
MAP L1

The Jardim do Torel is a less well known viewpoint, a small garden on a slope overlooking Restauradores and the Avenida da Liberdade. It provides not just a fine view of the city, but a great place for quiet contemplation, too.

10 Arco da Rua Augusta
MAP M5

This impressively ornate arch dominates the north side of Praça do Comércio. It was built as a gateway to the reconstructed city following the 1755 earthquake, with the statues at the top representing Portuguese figures from history. Take a lift and a narrow spiral staircase to the top of the arch for stunning views over downtown Baixa. On the way back down, you can visit the Clock Room, an exhibition space alongside the workings of the original 19th-century clock.

Parque Eduardo VII's unbroken vista

🔟 Beaches

1 Caparica Norte
South of Lisbon, the Caparica coast is busiest at its northern end, where you'll find Caparica town, plus an assortment of mid-range hotels, holiday homes, camp sites and restaurants.

2 Caparica Centre
Further south, the Caparica beach gets less busy, but has fewer amenities. From late spring to early autumn the Transpraia train runs from Caparica town to Fonte da Telha, stopping at bars and restaurants en route. The beach at Fonte da Telha is great for families, but note that many facilities are closed out of season.

3 Carcavelos
The broadest and longest beach along the Estoril coast is far enough from Lisbon for clean water and yet close enough for an afternoon outing. Beachside bars and restaurants provide ample opportunity for meals and refreshments. This is an excellent surfing area, and there are a number of surf schools at the beach. Carcavelos is still extremely pleasant out of season.

4 Estoril and Cascais
These beaches get very crowded, as they are mostly short and narrow. Still, the promenade that runs just above them, all the way from Estoril to Cascais, is full of relaxed bars and restaurants, where you can also take in the sun.

Clifftop view of Adraga beach

5 Adraga
Beyond Cabo da Roca, this pretty beach is reached via Almoçageme, off the Sintra road. Sintra's cooler climate prevails in this area. There's just one restaurant, but it is excellent.

6 Guincho
Guincho can provide an eyeful of sand on a windy day, but experienced surfers love it and it is the least developed of all the beaches along the Estoril coast. Beyond the built-up outskirts of Cascais, and with the Sintra hills as a backdrop, Guincho is a magnificent spot, and it draws the crowds on summer weekends. To avoid parking hassles, rent a

The beach and promenade along the coast at Estoril

bicycle in Cascais and ride out on the track that runs alongside the spectacular coast road.

7 Grande

With the longest unbroken stretch of sand in the area, Grande is popular with surfers and body-boarders. There are also plenty of bars and restaurants, and one hotel.

8 Lagoa de Albufeira and Meco

The southern half of the Caparica coast is accessible only by driving towards Sesimbra. Lagoa de Albufeira is a lagoon popular with kite-surfers. Further south, Meco is backed by a village with restaurants and bars.

9 Das Maçãs

"Apple Beach" is one of the most family-friendly along the Sintra-Colares coast. There are lots of good seafood restaurants nearby.

Towering cliffs at secluded Ursa

10 Ursa

Not marked on maps and requiring a steep walk on narrow paths, Ursa is one of the most secluded beaches in the region. Surrounded by towering cliffs like giants seated in the surf, it has no amenities, and anything beyond a short dip close to shore is not advisable. The beach is reached along the road to Cabo da Roca, where there is a small sign marked Ursa. Park your car out of sight of the road and head down the path.

TOP 10 OUTDOOR ACTIVITIES

Mountain biking in Arrábida

1 Walking
For dirt rather than cobbles underfoot, head for Sintra, Arrábida or the area surrounding the Tejo estuary.

2 Cycling
Cycling is becoming increasingly popular in Lisbon, and bikes can be rented in Cascais and near Belém.

3 Board Sports
Surfing and body-boarding are big along the Estoril and Sintra coasts, as is kite-surfing on the Caparica coast.

4 Fishing
Fishermen seem to be all along the river and beaches. Tourists hoping to cast out a line can take organized boat trips off the coast of Cascais.

5 Bird-watching
The Tagus marshlands beyond Alcochete and the Tróia peninsula are rich in bird life almost all year round.

6 Sailing
There are sailing schools in Parque das Nações, Belém and along the Estoril coast. Renting larger craft is possible.

7 Horse Riding
There are a number of *equestre* or *hípico* clubs around Cascais and Sintra, and at Belas nearer Lisbon.

8 Jogging
The western riverfront is reasonable jogging territory, as is Parque Eduardo VII. Monsanto and the Guincho coast are other options.

9 Mountain Biking
Lisbon's hills and cobbled streets provide ideal terrain for mountain biking. For country biking, head to the tracks around Sintra or Arrábida.

10 Roller Skating
Parque das Nações, the Alcântara docks and Belém all have areas suitable for skating.

🔟 Off the Beaten Track

The Cristo Rei monument and shrine towers over Lisbon

1 Cristo Rei
Almada ▪ 212 751 000
▪ 9:30am–6:45pm daily (Oct–Jun to 6pm) ▪ www.cristorei.pt

From his perch on the south side of the river, Christ the King overlooks Lisbon. The 28-m (92-ft) statue on its 82-m (270-ft) pedestal was inaugurated in 1959, in thanks for Portugal's escape from involvement in World War II. Inspired by the famous statue in Rio de Janeiro, it has since become an important site of pilgrimage. Lifts ascend to the platform at the foot of the statue.

2 Almada
The characterful old centre of this city offers fine views back over Lisbon. Take the modern lift, Elevador da Boca do Vento, to the attractive riverside strip of Jardim do Rio.

Prazeres tomb

3 Cacilhas
Catch the ferry for the fun ride to this little port opposite Lisbon, which is home to some terrific fish restaurants, as well as the *Don Fernando II e Glória*, a restored 19th-century frigate that is now a museum.

4 Prazeres
MAP D4 ▪ Praça São João Bosco ▪ 213 961 511 ▪ 9am–5:30pm daily (Oct–Apr to 4:30pm) ▪ www.cm-lisboa.pt

Take tram 28 to nearly the end of the line to visit Lisbon's main cemetery, a neatly laid-out village of pristine tombs. This tranquil spot is where some of Lisbon's most important inhabitants have been buried, among some of Iberia's oldest cypress trees.

5 Praça das Amoreiras
MAP E3

Locals like to sit drinking coffee at a kiosk under the trees in this hidden-away square, complete with children's play area. The space is flanked by the arches of the last stretches of the 18th-century Aqueduto das Águas Livres, which brought water to the capital.

View of Almada city

6 Aqueduto das Águas Livres

If you have a head for heights, you can walk across the top of the most dramatic part of Lisbon's extraordinary aqueduct (see p86–7). It was built over a decade before the 1755 earth-quake – which it survived, continuing to supply water to a shattered city. Head for the section that crosses the Alcântara Valley. Some of the arches here are over 64 m (210 ft) high, and were the tallest stone arches in the world at the time they were built.

7 Palácio das Necessidades

MAP D5 ■ Largo das Necessidades ■ Gardens: 8am–7pm Mon–Fri, 10am–7pm Sat & Sun (Oct–Mar closes one hour earlier) ■ www.cm-lisboa.pt

This charming 18th-century palace was built by Dom João V and used by Portuguese royals until 1910. It now belongs to the Foreign Ministry. The interior is closed to the public, but the exotic gardens are delightful.

Palácio das Necessidades

8 Lapa
MAP E5

Set on a steep hillside overlooking the Tejo (or Tagus, in English), Lapa is the city's most desirable district. This is an area of lavish villas and mansions occupied by embassies, consulates and the rich. It's a great place to stroll, past tempting cafés and exclusive restaurants.

9 Poço dos Negros Area

MAP F4 ■ Rua do Poço dos Negros/Rua de São Bento/Rua dos Poiais de São Bento

This part of Lisbon was once linked with the slave trade. Later it became a Little Cape Verde, where men from the islands stayed while seeking work. Most have moved to the suburbs with their families, but the area still has Cape Verdean restaurants and shops.

10 Barbadinhos Steam Pumping Station

Rua do Alviela 12 ■ **218 100 215** ■ 10am–12:30pm, 1:30–5:30pm Tue–Sat ■ www.epal.pt

This fascinating relic of Victorian ingenuity was built in 1880 to pump water from a nearby reservoir up Lisbon's steep hills. It worked non-stop until 1928. The museum also hosts temporary exhibits.

TOP 10 Activities for Children

Sharks cruising underwater at Oceanário

1 Monsanto
MAP B2

Monsanto (see p86) is a pine wood located on the city's western fringes. The Parque Recreativo do Alto da Serafina and Parque Infantil do Alvito are both popular, fenced-off, well-equipped play areas.

2 Jardim Zoológico
MAP D1 ■ Praça Marechal Humberto Delgado ■ 21 Mar–20 Sep: 10am–8pm daily; 21 Sep–20 Mar: 10am–6pm daily (last adm 1 hr & 15 mins before closing) ■ Adm

Lisbon's zoo is loved by children of all ages. One of the most popular features is an open-air cable car, which allows you a bird's-eye view of many of the animal enclosures. Other attractions include a train and an excellent reptile house.

Meeting giraffes at Lisbon Zoo

3 Oceanário
Opened for the 1998 Lisbon Expo, the Oceanário (see p20) remains the biggest single attraction in Parque das Nações. The second-largest aquarium in the world, it holds an impressive array of species.

4 Knowledge Pavilion – Ciência Viva

This hands-on science museum (see p21) has vast halls full of intriguing gadgetry to illustrate the fundamental laws of nature, as well as more exotic phenomena. Downstairs, the youngest visitors get the chance to don hard hats and help build the Unfinished House.

5 Quinta Pedagógica
MAP C1 ■ Rua Cidade de Lobito ■ May–Sep: 9am–7pm Tue–Fri, 10am–7pm Sat & Sun; Oct–Apr: 9am–5:30pm Tue–Fri, 10am–5:30pm Sat & Sun

This city farm offers the chance to handle baby animals and to learn about rural activities and crafts.

6 Roller Skating, Ice Skating and Skateboarding

There are several places in Lisbon with ramps and rinks for roller skating and skateboarding. One of the best is by the Vasco da Gama tower in Parque das

Nações *(see p20)*. In winter, an outdoor ice rink is erected in Parque Eduardo VII *(see p95)*.

7 Swimming Pools

Many hotels have outdoor pools. The Clube Nacional de Natação has a complex with indoor and outdoor pools at Rua de São Bento 209, or try the Olaias Clube at Rua Robalo Gouveia in east Lisbon.

8 Museu da Electricidade

MAP B6 ■ Avenida de Brasilia ■ 10am–6pm Tue–Sun

Located on Lisbon's waterfront, the Electricity Museum includes a hands-on section where children can play and learn.

Museu da Electricidade exhibit

9 Beaches

The Atlantic is not the safest water for young ones to play in. Low tide is a good time for building sand castles and paddling in pools left by the receding sea. Some of the beaches along the Estoril coast *(see p44)* are more protected; or head for Portinho de Arrábida or Tróia *(see pp58–9)*.

10 Museu Nacional de História Natural e da Ciência

MAP J2 ■ Rua da Escola Politécnica 58 ■ 10am–5pm Tue–Fri, 11am–6pm Sat & Sun (closed Sun in Jul & Aug) ■ Adm

Housed in the grand setting of the old Polytechnic, this science and natural history museum by the Jardim Botânico *(see pp84–5)* has an engaging hands-on exhibit illustrating the basic principles of physics.

TOP 10 FAMILY-FRIENDLY RESTAURANTS

Nosolo Itália treats

1 Casanova
A popular quay-side pizzeria with a safe veranda; kids can watch the chef at work *(see p67)*.

2 31 da Armada
Praça da Armada 31 ■ 213 976 330
Plus points at this place include the traffic-free square and friendly staff.

3 Nosolo Itália
A tempting array of pizzas, pastas and ice creams are served on a large outdoor terrace *(see p89)*.

4 Café Buenos Aires
The steps outside are traffic-free; inside, the vibe is friendly *(see p83)*.

5 Psi
The pretty gardens surrounding this restaurant are perfect for children to play in *(see p99)*.

6 Papagaio da Serafina
Parque Recreativo do Alto da Serafina ■ 217 743 021
A pavilion-style restaurant with an ambitious menu in Monsanto's best children's park.

7 Jardim dos Sentidos
Rua da Mãe d'Água 3 ■ 213 423 670
Vegetarian food is served here in a lovely space with an interior garden.

8 Restaurants at Doca de Santo Amaro
Doca de Santo Amaro
Facing a marina, these family-friendly restaurants have outdoor tables.

9 Restaurants in Parque das Nações
Parque das Nações
Choices range from food courts to riverside terraces and steak houses.

10 Restaurants along Rua Vieira Portuense, Belém
This is a short street of outdoor restaurants overlooking the Jardim de Belém *(see p88)*.

🔟 Bars and Nightclubs

Colourful bar area at Station

1 Station
MAP F5 ■ Cais do Gás, Armazém A

An appealing mix of soul and techno can be enjoyed at this waterfront club. There's a very good restaurant on the ground floor.

2 Main
MAP E5 ■ Avenida 24 de Julho 68

Spread across three floors, Main also houses a traditional Portuguese restaurant. The club draws its energy from a wide-ranging crowd of revellers.

3 K Urban Beach
MAP E5 ■ Cais da Viscondessa, Rua da Cintura ■ Wed–Sat

This modern entertainment complex features three dance floors, a succession of guest DJs, two restaurants and a pool terrace.

Clubgoers at Lux

With a prime riverside location in Santos, this club has some of the best views in Lisbon.

4 Lux
MAP R3 ■ Cais da Pedra, Avenida Infante Dom Henrique

Lux is considered Lisbon's most stylish and varied nightclub. With a downstairs dance floor, an upstairs bar and dance area, a rooftop terrace, groovy retro decor and a string of hot DJs, it lives up to the hype.

5 Bar Lounge
MAP J5 ■ Rua da Moeda 1

Resident disc-spinner Mário Valente has been working to enrich Bar Lounge's eclectic mix of indie and electronic pop and rock since the early noughties. Located down an alley, Bar Lounge has a full programme of live bands that, combined with a relaxed atmosphere, has earned it a loyal following.

6 Europa Sunrise
MAP K6 ■ Pátio do Pinzaleiro 26, Cais do Sodré

This venue offers an eclectic mix of popular club anthems and alternative favourites for night owls. The club is open from 5am to 10am on Saturdays, Sundays and public holidays.

7 Incógnito
MAP F4 ■ Rua dos Poiais de São Bento 37

This veteran of the early 1990s has kept on doing what it does best and

draws a mostly low-profile crowd. Somewhere between a bar and a club, it accommodates both chill-out areas and a dance floor. The music is a mixed bag, with recent dance sounds on weeknights and a broader spectrum at weekends.

8 Ministerium
MAP G5 ■ Terreiro do Paço, Ala Nascente 72–73

This stylish nightclub, with a large dance floor and bar, boasts one of the best locations in town, plus music from some of the world's top DJs. Comfortable chairs have been set up in corners for an occasional retreat from the music, which veers towards techno and electronica. Open only on Saturdays.

Lively Rua Nova do Carvalho

9 Rua Nova do Carvalho (Pink Street)
MAP K6

Once the sort of street to avoid after dark, this has now been cleaned up and rebranded as "Pink Street", thanks to the alarming colour of the road. The result: one of the hippest streets in which to spend the evening. Old dance clubs such as Jamaica are still to be found, alongside trendy bars such as Povo, Sol e Pesca and the club/music venue Music Box.

10 Dock's Club
MAP D5 ■ Rua da Cintura do Porto ■ Tue, Fri & Sat

A well-established dance venue on West Lisbon's waterfront, Dock's Club has a ladies' night every Tuesday. The club hosts live music on Fridays, and the popular Saturday Night Fever takes place the following night.

TOP 10 FADO VENUES

Parreirinha de Alfama

1 Clube de Fado
Rua de São João da Praça 94 ■ 218 852 704
This essential Alfama *fado* venue, owned by *guitarrista* Mário Pacheco, showcases new stars.

2 Parreirinha de Alfama
Beco do Espírito Santo 1 ■ 218 868 209
A traditional venue owned by the famous singer Argentina Santos.

3 Senhor Vinho
Rua do Meio à Lapa 18 ■ 213 972 681
Quality and style characterize the singing at this expensive restaurant.

4 Timpanas
Rua Gilberto Rola 24 ■ 213 906 655
Timpanas offers a superb dinner show with first-class *fado*.

5 Tasca do Chico
Rua dos Remédios 83 ■ 965 059 670
The place to see gritty *fado vadio*: amateur impromptu performances.

6 Café Luso
Travessa da Queimada 10 ■ 213 422 281
Offering first-class *fado* and fine food in the Bairro Alto since the 1920s.

7 Sr Fado
Rua dos Remédios 176 ■ 218 874 298
Warm and friendly venue with some of the best *fado* performers in town.

8 A Severa
Rua das Gáveas 51 ■ 218 428 314
An atmospheric venue named after the famous 19th-century gypsy *fadista*.

9 Casa de Linhares
Beco dos Armazéns do Linho 2 ■ 218 865 088
The *fado* side of a *bacalhau* restaurant.

10 O Faia
Rua da Barroca 54 ■ 213 426 742
One of Bairro Alto's larger venues, with good music and expensive food.

🔟 Restaurants

Contemporary decor at Bica do Sapato

1 Bica do Sapato
MAP R3 ▪ Avenida Infante Dom Henrique/Cais da Pedra, Armazém B ▪ 218 810 320 ▪ Closed Sun D & Mon L ▪ €€

Bica do Sapato manages to stay ahead of many newer contemporary restaurants in Lisbon. Downstairs there is a bar and a dining room; upstairs a sushi restaurant. Fish is the thing here – the restaurant is famous for its seafood stews.

2 Real Fábrica
MAP F3 ▪ Rua da Escola Politécnica 275 ▪ 213 852 090 ▪ Closed Sun ▪ €

This well-established restaurant, located just off Largo do Rato, is spread across two floors. The emphasis is on traditional Portuguese cuisine, with the grilled fish being a speciality. The restaurant also offers home-made desserts and an extensive wine list.

3 Espaço Lisboa
MAP D5 ▪ Rua da Cozinha Económica 16 ▪ 213 610 210 ▪ Closed L; Sun ▪ €€

Espaço Lisboa serves traditional Portuguese cuisine in a stylish environment. There's a good choice of fish options, as you might expect, plus classic meat dishes, such as veal in port wine.

4 A Travessa
MAP F5 ▪ Travessa do Convento das Bernardas 12 ▪ 213 902 034 ▪ Closed Sun, L Mon–Sat ▪ €€€

In the grand surroundings of an old convent (shared with private residents and a puppet museum), this welcoming restaurant feels like it could be in a provincial town. The food, though, is cosmopolitan, successfully mixing Portuguese, Belgian and French influences.

5 Tavares
MAP L4 ▪ Rua da Misericórdia 37 ▪ 213 421 112 ▪ Closed Sun ▪ €€€

A cavern of gilt, stucco and heavy mirrors, Tavares, which opened in 1784, claims to be Lisbon's oldest restaurant; the impressive decor, though, is early 20th-century. The fortunes of this restaurant have fluctuated, but you can rely on creative Portuguese cuisine from its tasting menu of five dishes.

6 Casa do Alentejo
MAP L2 ▪ Rua das Portas de Santo Antão 58 (upstairs) ▪ 213 405 140 ▪ €€

Overlooking a wonderful Moorish-style interior courtyard, this "embassy of the Alentejo region"

Tiled interior at Casa do Alentejo

is one of Lisbon's most memorable dining locations. Stick to soups, rice dishes or fish, and you won't forget the food either.

7 Eleven

MAP E2 ■ Rua Marquês da Fronteira, Jardim Amália Rodrigues ■ 213 862 211 ■ Closed Sun ■ €€€

A modernist window box at the top of Parque Eduardo VII is the setting for Lisbon's most sophisticated contemporary restaurant. Joachim Koerper is the chef behind the meticulously prepared food.

Beautifully presented food at Eleven

8 Chefe Cordeiro

MAP M5 ■ Praça do Comércio 20–23 ■ 216 080 090 ■ €€

Specialities at this restaurant include *bacalhau à Lisbonense* (Lisbon-style salt cod). There is an extensive wine list, and lovely outdoor seating.

9 Solar dos Presuntos

MAP L2 ■ Rua das Portas de Santo Antão 150 ■ 213 424 253 ■ Closed Sun ■ €€€

A traditional restaurant known for its *presunto* (cured ham) as well as other superb meat and seafood dishes. It also has a good selection of wines. Reservations recommended.

10 Restaurante 33

MAP F3 ■ Rua Alexandre Herculano 33A ■ 213 546 079 ■ Closed Sat L, Sun ■ €€

Enjoy Portuguese cuisine at this charming restaurant with al fresco dining. The desserts are divine.

TOP 10 CAFÉS AND PASTELARIAS

Confeitaria Nacional

1 Antiga Confeitaria de Belém
The birthplace of the original *pastel de nata* is a must for pastry enthusiasts.

2 Confeitaria Nacional
There are always queues for the pastries at this Lisbon institution – a sure sign of quality (see p74).

3 Bénard
For cakes, this is a much better option than the famous but crowded A Brasileira next door (see p81).

4 Pastelaria Suiça
A classy but affordable café with outdoor tables on both Rossio and Praça da Figueira (see p74).

5 Leitaria Caneças
Rua Bernardino Costa 36
Located near the British Bar (see p74), this quality bakery and pastry shop is also a popular café.

6 Café Mexicana
This classic Lisbon café-restaurant and social club is big and busy (see p99).

7 Pastelaria Versailles
Dream your way back to a time before fast food in this unreformed relic of old Lisbon (see p99).

8 Panificação Mecânica
Rua Silva Carvalho 209–25
This bakery and pastry shop, named after its early use of machinery, is an Art Nouveau jewel serving tasty treats.

9 Pão de Canela
Praça das Flores 27
This pleasant café has a terrace on quaint Praça das Flores. Children can play safely nearby.

10 Café Infusão
MAP L4 ■ Rua da Trindade 7
Popular for its teas, herbal infusions and the best pancakes in Lisbon.

For a key to restaurant price ranges see p67

Shopping Districts

① Baixa
MAP M4–5

The charm of the Baixa lies with its courteous shopkeepers, some of whom still stand behind wooden counters and do sums on bits of paper. For all that, the pedestrianized Rua Augusta is lined with modern chains.

Shop-lined Rua Augusta, Baixa

② Chiado
MAP L4

Traditionally the quarter with Lisbon's most elegant shops, the Chiado is now the city's most varied shopping area. It mixes quiet streets with lively squares and sheet-music suppliers with street-cred fashion boutiques.

③ Avenidas Guerra Junqueiro/Roma
MAP G1

Head to Avenida Guerra Junqueiro and adjacent Avenida Roma for good clothes shops and cafés – and a visit to the Campo Pequeno bullring. There is also a shopping complex nearby where several boutiques and delicatessens can be found.

④ Fresh Food Markets
MAP K6, E3, F2

Prices at Lisbon's food markets may not be lower than in the supermarkets, but the produce is often fresher and the experience is much more rewarding.

Mercado da Ribeira

Among the best are Mercado da Ribeira, opposite Cais do Sodré station; Mercado de Campo de Ourique, in west Lisbon; and Mercado 31 de Janeiro, behind the Saldanha Residence building on Avenida Fontes Pereira de Melo.

⑤ Campo de Ourique/Amoreiras
MAP E3

Gentrification proceeds at a gentle pace in Campo de Ourique. The grid street plan makes for lots of corner bakeries, cafés and small shops. Nearby, the brash Amoreiras Towers, Lisbon's first shopping centre, still provides plenty to tempt shoppers.

⑥ Rua de São Bento/Rua da Escola Politécnica
MAP F4

Rua de São Bento is a mini-district specializing in antiques and second-hand shops. It's a short hop to pleasant Praça das Flores for a coffee under the trees, and then an uphill walk to Rua da Escola Politécnica, and a cluster of more expensive antiques shops.

⑦ Avenida da Liberdade
MAP F3

Lisbon's main avenue, rising from the Baixa to the Parque Eduardo VII, has become the country's prime slice of real estate. It is lined with shops owned by upmarket designer brands, including Cartier, Gucci, Armani, Hugo Boss and Prada.

Bairro Alto clothes shop

8 Bairro Alto
MAP K3–4

Like the big shopping centres, Bairro Alto offers night-time shopping, but in a much cooler setting, and with the option of sipping a drink as you shop. Some stores seem ineffably trendy, but Bairro Alto is a nursery for Portuguese fashion and design.

9 Santa Apolónia
MAP R3

Although just a row of converted warehouses, this small shopping area opposite Santa Apolónia station has some of Lisbon's most interesting shops for music, food and design. The Bica do Sapato restaurant *(see p52)* is nearby.

Feira da Ladra bargains

10 Feira da Ladra
MAP Q2 ▪ Campo de Santa Clara ▪ 9am–3pm Tue & Sat

Lisbon's Thieves' Market sells quirky items such as beautiful brass taps that won't fit any known plumbing system. As with most flea markets, it's all about the sights and sounds, the people and the haggling.

TOP 10 THINGS TO BUY

1 Ceramics
Portuguese ceramics extend from tiles to pottery, and from rustic to twee.

2 Embroidery
Bordados are delicate, but long-lasting, old-world table linen.

3 Clothes at Markets
Rifle through rails of fakes and failures for the odd find at Cascais on the first or third Sunday of the month, or Carcavelos on any Thursday.

4 Shoes
Fewer shoes are made in Portugal now, but those that are tend to be of a very high quality.

5 Stainless Steel Cookware
There are several good-value brands of pots, pans and other kitchen essentials. Look out for Artame and Lourenço.

6 Wine
A wisely spent €5 will get you a truly good wine; €20 an unforgettable one. The wide choice is a pleasant surprise.

7 Cheese
Choose from runny Serra ewe's milk cheeses, delicious Serpa and Azeitão, peppery Castelo Branco and excellent hard and soft goat's cheeses.

8 Hams and Smoked Meats
The best *presunto* (cured ham) is from the north, but the Alentejan ham of the Ibérico pig is arguably better. Taste first, and decide for yourself.

9 Preserved Foods
Sardines and other tinned fish, olives, olive oil, *massa de pimentão* (red-pepper paste) and chilli sauce are all superb and readily available.

10 Beauty Treatments
Lisbon's beauty salons are labour-intensive rather than high-tech and offer good value.

Wine shop

Lisbon for Free

Seafront promenade at Cascais

1 Cascais Coast

Lisbon is close to some fantastic stretches of beach. Head to Estoril and you can walk up the seafront promenade to Cascais, past several sandy beaches *(see p101)*.

2 Museu da Electricidade

MAP B6 ■ Avenida de Brasilia, Belém ■ 210 028 130 ■ 10am–6pm Tue–Sun

Once one of the city's principal sources of electricity, the Central Tejo power station became a museum in 1990. It has an interactive exhibition which enables kids to take part in various hands-on experiments.

3 Riverside Walk

MAP D6–A6

The riverside is largely traffic-free from the Doca de Santo Amaro to the Torre de Belém, making for a lovely stroll past the dramatic Ponte 25 de Abril and Belém's monuments.

The riverside Torre de Belém

4 Museu do Design e da Moda (MUDE)

Anyone interested in design or fashion will want to linger at this tremendous collection of classics from the 1930s onwards, set in a former bank. Visitors can explore some of the world's very best examples of 20th-century furniture, haute couture, street fashion and more *(see p38)*.

5 Núcleo Arqueológico da Rua dos Correeiros

Phone ahead to book a fascinating free guided tour that takes you below the Millennium BCP bank in Baixa *(see p70)*. Builders uncovered ancient remains here while working on the bank in the 1990s, and excavations have revealed Roman fish-preserving tanks, Moorish ceramics and Christian graves.

Display of finds from beneath a bank at the Núcleo Arqueológico

6 Museu Coleção Berardo

MAP A6 ■ Praça do Império, Belém ■ 213 612 878 ■ 10am–7pm daily ■ www.museuberardo.pt

There are around 1,000 works at this free-to-enter museum of modern art, from canvas and sculpture to video installations from the likes of Francis Bacon, Peter Blake, Marc Chagall, Anish Kapoor and Man Ray.

7 Festival for Santo António

MAP H4 ■ Alfama

On 12–13 June, Lisbon celebrates its main saint's day. There are free

Evening parade during the annual Santo António festival

daytime parades and most districts have evening street parties with food stalls and dancing. The Alfama is the best place to head if you want to join in the festivities.

 Free Entry to Major Museums

Many of Lisbon's top attractions have free entry periods, including the Museu Calouste Gulbenkian (see pp30–31) which is free every Sunday; and the Museu Nacional de Arte Antiga (see pp18–19), Mosteiro dos Jerónimos (see pp14–15), Torre de Belém (see pp22–3) and the Palácio da Ajuda (see p88), all free on the first Sunday of every month.

 Feira da Ladra

Lisbon's rambling flea market is as good for people-watching as it is for finding the odd bargain among a panoply of clothes, antiques, crafts and people's cast-offs. Get there when the market opens to spot the most interesting characters and items.

10 Rua Augusta

The broad, pedestrianized main street through the Baixa usually offers plenty of free entertainment, from living statues to mime artists. Look out for the triumphal arch at the end of the street (see p69).

TOP 10 MONEY-SAVING TIPS

1 For travel to the outlying sights, buy a one-day (€6) or a three-day (€13.50) travel pass, which allow unlimited access to buses, the metro and trams.

2 You can explore all of central Lisbon on foot. Make sure you have sturdy shoes to negotiate its many hills.

3 There are inexpensive bike hire outfits on the riverfront at Belém and in Cascais; cycling is the best way to explore these relatively flat districts.

4 Locals spend whole days at the giant shopping centres such as Amoreiras (see p54), Centro Colombo (see p98) or Centro Vasco da Gama in the Parque das Nações (see pp20–21). Along with shops and supermarkets, they boast some of the city's least expensive cafés and fast-food outlets.

5 Check for free festivals, concerts or events on the city's listings website, www.agendalx.pt.

6 The Lisboa Card (€18.50 for one day, €31.50 for two days, €39 for three days), available from tourist offices, allows free travel on public transport and admission to 25 major sights around the city.

7 Take advantage of the good-value set meals in cafés and restaurants, particularly at lunchtime.

8 It's normal to be offered an array of starters when you sit down in a restaurant, but you'll pay for anything you eat. Politely decline anything you don't want.

9 You'll save money by ordering a drink from the counter or bar of a café rather than taking a seat and being served by a waiter.

10 Take the cheaper passenger ferry from Cais do Sodré to Cacilhas across the Tejo; it's a shorter ride than a boat trip, but the views are just as good.

Cycling in Lisbon's streets

🔟 Excursions

1 Sintra Hills
The romantic beauty of Sintra (see pp32–3) and its palaces – the crumbling walls veiled with moss, the views, the winding roads under dense canopies of leaves – all combine to make a visit to the Sintra hills a magical experience.

2 Serra da Arrábida
This limestone massif, about 40 minutes south of Lisbon by car, provides Portugal with its Mediterranean-like scenery – calm, blue-green waters and dramatic cliffs. Head for Portinho da Arrábida, and stop frequently to admire the views as you get close.

3 Alcácer do Sal
The ancient town of Alcácer do Sal (al-kasr from the Arabic for castle, and do sal from its trade in salt) sits peacefully on the north bank of the River Sado. Here you can enjoy the views from the 6th-century castle (now a pousada) and relax in the pleasant cafés along the riverside promenade.

4 Palmela and Azeitão
The main sight in Palmela is its hilltop castle, now an elegant pousada, which is open to passing visitors. Vila Fresca de Azeitão and Vila Nogueira de Azeitão are neighbouring towns at the heart of Palmela wine country.

Flamingoes on the Tróia peninsular

5 Setúbal and Tróia
The port town of Setúbal is prosaic, but it is home to the Igreja de Jesus, the first and perhaps most distinctive example of the Manueline style. People and cars are ferried across the mouth of the Sado river to the Tróia peninsula, which has excellent beaches extending south, and its estuary side is a haven for birds.

6 Tejo Estuary
Referred to in English as the Tagus, the estuary is accessible from Lisbon via Alcochete, just across the Vasco da Gama bridge. From here you can drive or walk into the lezíria marshlands, one of Europe's most important staging sites for migrating water birds, including flamingo, black-tailed godwit and avocet.

Hilltop castle, Palmela

7 Óbidos

Óbidos is arguably the most picturesque town in Portugal. Contained within the walls of a 14th-century castle, it is filled with whitewashed houses with their edges painted ochre or blue, and their windows adorned with lace curtains and potted geraniums. The town was the wedding gift of Dom Dinis to his queen, Isabel of Aragon, in 1282.

8 Mafra

Mafra is home to an extravagant palace and monastery built for Dom João V, Portugal's 18th-century monarch, who had a weakness for excess of all kinds. The almost pyramidal proportions of its construction are entertainingly detailed in José Saramago's novel *Baltasar and Blimunda*. A section of Mafra's hunting grounds is now used for a wolf conservation project.

Palace interior at Mafra

9 Vila Franca de Xira

A centre for bullfighting, this town hosts the Festa do Colete Encarnado in July every year, a raucous and showy festival that includes bull-running. A similar festival, the Feira do Outubro, takes place in October.

10 Ribatejo Wine Route

Some of the best wine producers in the Ribatejo region are clustered on the left bank of the Tejo, just north of Vila Franca de Xira, particularly between the towns of Almeirim and Alpiarça. Most welcome visitors. Seek out Quinta do Casal Branco, Quinta da Alorna, Fiuza & Bright and Quinta da Lagoalva de Cima.

TOP 10 BEAUTY SPOTS

Palace-pavillion at Monserrate

1 Guincho Coast
Cars drive very slowly – a rare thing in Portugal – along this beautifully scenic coast road (see p101).

2 Castelo dos Mouros
The steeply stepped walls of this attractive 8th-century castle offer some really fabulous views.

3 Penedo
This village on the high road from Sintra to the coast is misty and romantic in winter and a cool refuge in summer.

4 Peninha
This small sanctuary offers views of Europe's western edge, plus a small group of buildings with an intriguing history (see p104).

5 Ursa
Stroll along this secluded beach out of season and take in the sheer beauty of the place (see p45).

6 Monserrate
With a history of English gardeners and visitors, the stunning gardens and palace-pavilion of Monserrate remain popular (see pp102–103).

7 Portinho da Arrábida
One of the most protected beaches along the western seaboard looks as though it belongs in Croatia or Turkey.

8 Pancas and Around
If you prefer huge skies and endless views, head for this hamlet northeast of Alcochete, on the edge of the *lezíria*.

9 Cabo Espichel
The clifftop southwesternmost point of the Setúbal peninsula is in some ways more attractive than the better known Cabo da Roca.

10 Bucelas and Beyond
For a taste of inland Estremadura – and some superb white wine.

Lisbon Area by Area

Keep entrance, Castelo de São Jorge

🔟 Alfama, Castelo and the East

Cloister, the Sé

Alfama's Arabic-sounding name recalls its past as an important district of Moorish Lisbon. No buildings survive from this era, but Alfama suffered little damage in the 1755 earthquake, so its medieval street plan has remained intact – and largely traffic-free. The Castelo neighbourhood at the top adjoins the higher hill district of Graça. To the south and east, Alfama descends to the river.

AREA MAP OF ALFAMA, CASTELO AND THE EAST

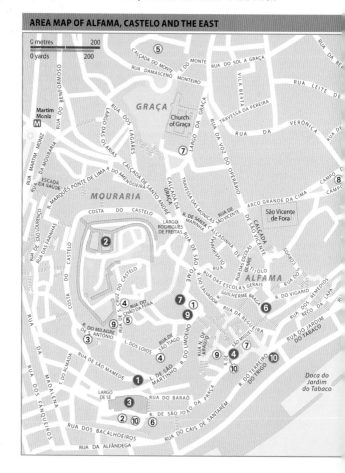

1 Museu do Teatro Romano

MAP N4 ■ Rua São Mamede 3
■ 217 513 200 ■ Open 10am–5pm
Tue–Sun

A Roman amphitheatre dating from the 1st century BC lies beneath the buildings just above the Sé. Not a lot has yet been excavated, but it seems to have been a sizable structure, with seating for up to 5,000. Excavations are ongoing, and visitors are offered an insight into the archaeological work that continues here, as well as at various other sites in central Lisbon.

Castelo de São Jorge and Alfama

2 Castelo de São Jorge

The castle that crowns Alfama was the heart of the city in the Moorish era, and the site goes back to Phoenician times at least *(see pp12–13)*. The picturesque residential area within the castle's outer walls is also called Castelo.

3 The Sé

The English crusader Gilbert of Hastings, Lisbon's first bishop, oversaw the construction of the city's cathedral in the mid-12th century. The site was previously occupied by a mosque, parts of which have been excavated *(see pp16–17)*.

4 Largo de São Miguel

MAP P4

You can reach this square in the heart of Alfama via steps from Largo das Portas do Sol; walk down next to Santa Luzia church and bear left after the first corner. This is the essence of Alfama: narrow alleys that older residents use as gardens, grills with sardines smoking, patios, archways and twisting stairs. The absence of cars lets children play everywhere. On 12 June every year, Largo de São Miguel is at the centre of the huge party thrown to honour St Anthony, Lisbon's most popular patron saint.

1	**Top 10 Sights**	see pp63–5
1	**Restaurants**	see p67
1	**Bars and Cafés**	see p66

5 Igreja de Santa Engrácia/Panteão Nacional

The soaring dome of Santa Engrácia is a landmark on Lisbon's low eastern skyline, but when you approach it on foot it seems to duck out of view at every turn. The dome was added as recently as 1966 – 284 years after the construction of the church began. This in turn has enriched the Portuguese language with a saying that translates as "a job like Santa Engrácia", for any interminable project. Built on a Greek cross plan with rounded arms, the church has similarities to St Peter's Basilica in Rome, although Santa Engrácia is even-sided. The airy, marble-clad interior serves as the National Pantheon (see p40).

6 Santo Estevão
MAP Q4

The small esplanade in front of the Santo Estevão church is one of the area's best viewing points. Access is easy, if steep, from Largo do Chafariz de Dentro, at the foot of Alfama, where you will find one of the city's oldest public fountains (as well as the Fado Museum, so you can easily combine a visit to both). Just head up Rua dos Remédios and climb the Escadas de Santo Estevão steps on your left.

7 Largo das Portas do Sol
MAP P4

When the 28 tram gets to the top of the hill beyond the Sé, it squeezes between two buildings in what used to be the Moorish-era city walls.

ST ANTHONY OF THE SARDINES

The celebration of St Anthony (**above**), on 12 June, falls close to the feast days of other saints (São João and São Pedro, or John and Peter), resulting in a two-week party known as the *Festas dos Santos Populares*. In fact, the city has declared the whole month *Festas da Cidade*. But the real party is in Largo de São Miguel on 12 June, when tables are set up everywhere, grills are fired up and loaded with sardines, the wine and beer flow freely and bands play.

This spot gives one of the best views of Alfama and the river. Backtrack past the Santa Luzia church, and you reach the Miradouro de Santa Luzia, one of the city's official viewpoints (see p42). Across the street are two access routes to the castle. There are several outdoor cafés in the area.

8 Museu Nacional do Azulejo

Beyond Alfama, in the eastern Xabregas district, is the Tile Museum (see pp26–7), housed in a stunning former 16th-century convent with an elaborately decorated church.

View from Largo das Portas do Sol

Highlights include a small Manueline cloister, a 23-m (75-ft) panel of painted tiles showing Lisbon in the 1740s, and extensive collections of Moorish and Portuguese tiles. The café-restaurant is a pleasant place to take a break.

⑨ Fundação Ricardo do Espírito Santo Silva

MAP P4 ▪ Largo das Portas do Sol 2 ▪ 218 881 991 ▪ 10am–5pm Wed–Mon ▪ Adm

Named after the banker who bequeathed a 17th-century Alfama palace filled with his collections of decorative arts, this museum displays an extensive collection of Portuguese, French and English furniture in period settings. Next door are workshops for traditional crafts such as cabinet-making, gilding and bookbinding. The foundation also runs two schools of arts and crafts in other locations.

Display at the Museu do Fado

⑩ Museu do Fado

MAP Q4 ▪ Largo do Chafariz do Dentro 1 ▪ 218 823 470 ▪ 10am–6pm Tue–Sun ▪ Adm

Also called the Casa do Fado e da Guitarra Portuguesa, this museum is dedicated to Lisbon's most famous musical genre and to the mandolin-shaped Portuguese guitar. This instrument, whose strings are in pairs, combines with the singer's soaring tremolos to give *fado* – often compared with the blues – its unique sound. The museum is surprisingly recent, but its life-size replica of a *fado* venue – complete with singer, musicians, staff and customers – has an old-fashioned feel.

ALFAMA WANDERING

▶ MORNING

Alfama is really the sort of place to wander around with an open mind rather than an open guidebook. Like most labyrinthine medieval quarters it is actually quite small, but it seems large to the first-time visitor. Here are a few pointers, to help you on your way. The street that begins on the right side of the Sé, briefly called **Cruzes da Sé** and then **Rua de São João da Praça**, is a good point of entry. There are also some worthwhile cafés and bars along here, including **Pois, Café** *(see p66)*. Don't turn right off this street, or you'll be led down and out of the maze. Instead, keep going and follow it round, and you'll eventually reach **Rua de São Pedro**, which leads down to **Largo do Chafariz de Dentro**, where there's a good choice of restaurants for lunch.

AFTERNOON

To return to the maze, head back up Rua de São Pedro and do a near 180-degree turn at the top to reach **Igreja de São Miguel**. Follow left turns by right turns and you should be able to weave your way to **Santo Estevão**. Should thirst overcome you, head down the steps to bar and restaurant **Pateo 13**. A brisk walk up Rua dos Remedios and then along Rua do Paraíso will get you to **Campo de Santa Clara** and, if it's Tuesday or Saturday, the **Feira da Ladra** *(see p55)*. If it's not, stroll down to the riverside row of converted warehouses at **Santa Apolónia** for another kind of shopping experience *(see p55)*.

See map on pp62–3 ←

Bars and Cafés

1 Portas do Sol
MAP P4 ▪ Largo das Portas do Sol

This stylish café, bar and restaurant is right by the Portas do Sol viewpoint. The lovely outdoor seating area affords splendid views of the Tejo estuary and beyond.

2 Cruzes Credo
MAP N5 ▪ Rua Cruzes da Sé 29

Deliciously cool on a summer's day, this jazzy café serves a range of drinks and snacks such as burgers, salads and tapas. Try a strong coffee with some fabulous chocolate cake.

Outdoor dining at Chapitô

3 Chapitô
MAP N4 ▪ Costa do Castelo 7

This large, friendly bar, café and restaurant offers a variety of seating areas and superb views.

4 Santiago Alquimista
MAP P4 ▪ Rua de Santiago 19

Set in the spacious basement of a drama school, this bar is at the vanguard of Lisbon's music and multicultural scene.

5 Café do Monte
MAP G3 ▪ Rua de São Gens 1

Food is served all day long at this café in the district of Graça. The artistic interiors conjure up a Parisian ambience.

6 Pois, Café
MAP P5 ▪ Rua de São João da Praça 93–5

This living-room-style café, with a cool but relaxed vibe, was the first of its kind in Lisbon when it was opened by its Austrian owners. *Pois* is a much-used Portuguese word that perhaps sounded quaint to Austrian ears.

7 Esplanada da Igreja da Graça
MAP P2 ▪ Largo da Graça

One of Lisbon's best café-table views is to be had from the esplanade by the vast Graça church *(see p41)*. It is particularly attractive in the late afternoon on a sunny day.

8 Deli Delux
MAP R3 ▪ Avenida Infante Dom Henrique/Cais da Pedra, Armazém B, Loja 8

This is a well-stocked deli with a café at the back and a small terrace. Its weekend brunches are great, but come early to avoid having to wait for a table.

9 Wine Bar do Castelo
MAP N4 ▪ Rua Bartolomeu de Gusmão 13

More than 150 Portuguese wines can be tasted here, along with a selection of meats and cheeses. A refreshing oasis right next to the castle.

10 Duetos da Sé
MAP P5 ▪ Travessa do Almargem 1b

Gastronomy meets art at this convivial café-bar behind the cathedral. Enjoy soups, sandwiches and snacks, often with live music.

Cool, cozy vibe at Pois, Café

Restaurants

PRICE CATEGORIES

For a three-course meal for one with half a bottle of wine (or equivalent meal), taxes and extra charges.

€ under €20 € €€ €20–€40 € €€€ over €40

① Bica do Sapato

In an airy space with fabulous river views, this modern restaurant also has a sushi bar upstairs. Trendy but not tediously so (see p52).

Stylish interior of Bica do Sapato

② Casanova

MAP R3 ▪ Avenida Infante Dom Henrique/Cais da Pedra, Armazém B, Loja 7 ▪ 218 877 532 ▪ €€

Lisbon's best pizzas are served at this lively restaurant with a terrace on the quay. Arrive early to avoid waiting.

③ D'Avis

MAP C2 ▪ Avenida Dom João II, Parque das Nações ▪ 218 681 354 ▪ Closed Sun ▪ €€

Well-prepared food from the Alentejo region is on the menu at this tavern. Try dishes of *porco preto*, flavourful free-range Iberian pig.

④ Casa do Leão

MAP N3 ▪ Castelo de São Jorge ▪ 218 875 962 ▪ €€€

Housed in the remains of the original Alcáçovas palace (see pp12–13), this grand restaurant serves an ambitious Portuguese menu. Sit outside, with Lisbon at your feet.

⑤ Arco do Castelo

MAP N4 ▪ Rua do Chão da Feira 25 ▪ 218 876 598 ▪ Closed Sun ▪ €€

Genuine Goan restaurants like this one are quite a rarity. Try specialities like *sarapatel* (a spicy stew made with meat, offal, blood and vinegar).

⑥ Faz Figura

MAP R3 ▪ Rua do Paraíso 15b ▪ 218 868 981 ▪ €€€

There are wonderful views of the river from the large terrace of this stylish international restaurant.

⑦ Lautasco

MAP Q4 ▪ Beco do Azinhal 7A (off Rua de São Pedro) ▪ 218 860 173 ▪ Closed Sun ▪ €€

Traditional Portuguese fare is the speciality of this informal restaurant, rustically decorated with wooden panelling.

⑧ Santa Clara dos Cogumelos

MAP Q2 ▪ Campo de Santa Clara 7 ▪ 218 870 661 ▪ Closed Sun, Mon, L Tue–Fri ▪ €€

There are splendid river views at this unassuming restaurant. Try the fried mushrooms in yogurt sauce.

⑨ Santo António de Alfama

MAP P4 ▪ Beco de São Miguel 7 ▪ 218 881 328 ▪ Open daily ▪ €€

Not as traditional as it sounds: the walls are lined with portraits of film stars, while the food is modern Portuguese and international.

⑩ A Baíuca

MAP H4 ▪ Rua de São Miguel 20 ▪ 218 867 284 ▪ Closed Tue, Wed, L ▪ €€

Among other options, this tiny restaurant serves up a delicious *bacalhau assado* (roasted salt cod). Amateur *fado* performances add to the traditional ambience.

See map on pp62–3 ←

TOP10 Baixa to Restauradores

From the early 16th to mid-18th centuries, Lisbon's royal palace stood on the riverbank, around today's Praça do Comércio. It was the grand entrance to Lisbon, one of the world's great cities. Then in 1755 the earth shook, the ocean rose and fires raged – and the Paço Real and most of the medieval jumble of buildings behind it were gone. The Baixa we see today was built on the ruins of lower Lisbon, to a different plan, in a different style, for a new era. Today this is the ageing heart of Lisbon, facing the challenges of depopulation, traffic, subsidence and new shopping centres – but still going strong.

Carving at Igreja da Conceição Velha

AREA MAP OF BAIXA TO RESTAURADORES

- **1** **Top 10 Sights**
  see pp69–71
- **1** **Restaurants**
  see p75
- **1** **Shops**
  see p73
- **1** **The Best of the Rest**
  see p72
- **1** **Bars and Cafés**
  see p74

Shoppers on Rua Augusta

reconstruction *(see p37)*, and facing the river along the fourth, this urban space is home to the Lisboa Story Centre, an exhibition hall, and several bars and restaurants. Dom José I, Portugal's ineffectual king at the time of the earthquake, gazes – perhaps fearfully – at the river from his horseback perch, in a bronze by Machado de Castro.

① Rua Augusta
MAP M4–5

Lisbon's longest and grandest pedestrianized street runs through the middle of Baixa, from one corner of Rossio to a triumphal archway on Praça do Comércio. The arch, which commemorates the city's recovery after the 1755 earthquake, was added only in 1873. An allegorical figure of Glory stands atop it, crowning with wreaths the figures representing Genius and Bravery. Below, a gallery of national heroes includes the Marquis of Pombal. The side of the arch facing Rua Augusta features a large clock, much consulted by the shoppers who throng the street.

② Praça do Comércio
MAP M5

The broad riverfront square also known as Terreiro do Paço has regained some of its stature since cars were prohibited from parking there. Surrounded on three sides by the elegant arcades of Pombal's

③ Igreja da Conceição Velha
MAP N5 ■ Rua da Alfândega
■ 9am–5pm Mon–Fri, 10am–2pm Sun, closed Sat

This was the grand 16th-century Igreja da Misericórdia before the 1755 earthquake, which destroyed everything but the Manueline portal and one interior chapel. When it opened again in 1770, it was taken over by the congregation of another Baixa church that had been irreparably damaged in the quake, the Conceição Velha. The new church was very modest, and most visitors today come to admire the detailed portal. This features a carved image of Our Lady of Mercy, her long mantle held by two angels to shelter kneeling historical figures including Dom Manuel, Pope Leo X and Dona Leonor, widow of João II and founder of the Misericórdia almshouses.

④ Igreja de São Domingos

Dark and cavernous, the São Domingos church *(see p40)* is not much visited by tourists, despite its long history. As a result, it is a good place for quiet reflection, whatever one's creed.

Statue and arch, Praça do Comércio

5 Núcleo Arqueológico da Rua dos Correeiros

MAP M4 ▪ Rua Augusta 96 ▪ 211 134 496 ▪ 10am–1pm & 2–5pm Mon–Sat ▪ Guided tours in English

When a Portuguese bank began renovating its head office in the early 1990s, builders uncovered ancient remnants of Roman Lisbon. A small museum was set up, and the digging goes on. So far, this has revealed parts of what appears to have been a factory for making *garum* (fermented fish sauce). A section of mosaic floor uncovered in a separate structure suggests other, or later, uses.

The Santa Justa lift

6 Elevador de Santa Justa

MAP M4 ▪ Rua de Santa Justa ▪ 7am–11pm summer, 7am–10pm winter daily ▪ Adm for ride/views

You may be told that this iron lift was designed by Gustave Eiffel (of Paris tower fame), but in fact it is by Raoul Mesnier de Ponsard, his Portuguese pupil. There were once three such lifts in Lisbon's craggy cityscape, before the dawn of small delivery lorries. Today the Neo-Gothic lift (check out the exterior walls of the tower) whisks locals and tourists from Baixa to the Carmo ruins *(see p77)*. There are photo opportunities and a scenic terrace at the top.

"ONLY THE PIGEONS WILL SEE IT ISN'T HIM…"

The statue atop the column in Rossio **(right)** represents Dom Pedro IV, who gave his name to the square. But it is said to be of Emperor Maximilian of Mexico, whose bronze likeness was in transit to Lisbon when news came of his assassination. Since the city fathers had just ordered a bronze of Dom Pedro IV from the same sculptor, agreement was reached to substitute, at a reduced price, the superfluous Maximilian.

7 Praça dos Restauradores

MAP L2

This plaza and its monument were built when the old Passeio Público was turned into Avenida da Liberdade in the 1870s. It commemorates the restoration of the Portuguese monarchy in 1640. The obelisk is engraved with important dates from the restoration campaign, and is flanked by statues representing the Spirit of Independence and Victory. The surrounding square is dominated by traffic; shops, cafés, kiosks and restaurants cluster in its lower corners.

Obelisk, Praça dos Restauradores

8 Rua das Portas de Santo Antão
MAP L2

This long, partly pedestrianized street has food choices galore. The legendary Gambrinus restaurant sits next to the tiny A Ginjinha bar, and between these extremes is a clutch of seafood restaurants with outdoor seating, plus the atmospheric Casa do Alentejo, the cheerful Bomjardim, and the inimitable Cervejaria Solmar (see p75).

Rua das Portas de Santo Antão

9 Praça da Figueira
MAP M3

After the earthquake, an open-air market was set up in what is now Praça da Figueira. It became the city's main vegetable market, eventually roofed with iron pavilions and cupolas. It joined next-door Rossio as Lisbon's bustling centre, scene of raucous Santo António celebrations in mid-June. It is today a shadow of its former self, serving as the roof of an underground car park. It looks quite attractive when viewed from the castle ramparts. There are broad, shaded café esplanades along one side.

10 Rossio
MAP L3–M3 ▪ Praça Dom Pedro IV

Rossio, officially Praça Dom Pedro IV, has been Lisbon's main square probably since Roman times. Surrounded by some of the city's grandest buildings before the earthquake, it was later outshone by the Praça do Comércio, but remains the city's cosmopolitan heart.

A STROLL THROUGH BAIXA

 MORNING

Begin at the riverside gardens to the west of **Praça do Comércio** (see p69), where the old palace steps can still be seen. Cross the square and admire the views from the top of **Rua Augusta** (see p69). Turning right on Rua da Alfândega, take in the Manueline portal of **Igreja da Conceição Velha**. Then head up Rua da Madalena, where you can drop into the **Conserveira de Lisboa** (see p72) for a souvenir of tinned sardines. Turn left at Largo da Madalena and descend two blocks to the narrower **Rua dos Douradoures**, where you will find plenty of options for lunch.

AFTERNOON

Work your way through Baixa's grid, up to the main pedestrianized Rua Augusta. Look out for Rua de Santa Justa and a view of the Elevador de Santa Justa. Next stop is the top left corner of **Praça da Figueira**, and a coffee at the back of **Pastelaria Suiça** (see p74). Then walk up **Rua Dom Antão de Almada**, past fragrant shops selling herbs and other dried goods. On your right is one of Lisbon's oldest churches, **Igreja de São Domingos** (see p40). Slightly left and then straight ahead is **Rua das Portas de Santo Antão**. If you've already worked up an appetite, you couldn't be in a better area; for a pre-prandial drink, duck into the **A Ginjinha** bar (see p74) for a cherry liqueur.

See map on p68

The Best of the Rest

Interior of the Teatro Nacional Dona Maria II

1 Elevador do Lavra
MAP L1 ▪ Largo da Anunciada/ Calçada do Lavra

The oldest Lisbon funicular, inaugurated in 1884, is the one most tourists overlook. Connecting Restauradores with Campo de Santana, it gets you to the Jardim do Torel viewpoint (see 43).

2 Rossio Station
MAP L3 ▪ Between Rossio and Restauradores squares

Built in 1892, the old central station now serves Sintra (see pp32–3). The statue in a niche between the horseshoe arches is of Dom Sebastião, the boy king lost in battle in 1578.

3 Shops in Rua do Arsenal
MAP L5

A whiff of an older Lisbon lives on in shops selling dried fish, from bacalhau (salt cod) to octopus, dried goods, wine and some fresh produce.

4 Haberdashers in Rua da Conceição
MAP M5 ▪ Between Rua Augusta and Rua da Prata

Baixa shopkeepers may be buckling under competition from the shopping centres, but at this string of haberdashers' shops you can still buy a single button or length of lace.

5 Teatro Nacional Dona Maria II
MAP L3 ▪ Praça Dom Pedro IV ▪ 213 250 800

The Neo-Classical building housing Portugal's national theatre was built around 1840, at the same time that Rossio was paved with its characteristic black and white cobblestones.

6 Centro Comercial Mouraria
MAP N2 ▪ Praça Martim Moniz ▪ 218 880 904 ▪ Open 9am–8pm Mon–Sat

A six-level hotchpotch of small stores, mostly selling ethnic food, clothes and accessories.

7 Antiga Ervanária d'Anunciada
MAP L2 ▪ Largo da Anunciada 13–15 ▪ 213 427 997

Claiming to be Portugal's oldest herbalist, this shop sells vitamin super-cures as well as traditional dried herbs for infusions.

8 Shoeshiners in Largo de São Domingos
MAP M3

The engraxador is a Lisbon figure much stereotyped in literature and film, but his is a fading trade. The surest place to find one is outside or in the A Ginjinha bar (see p74). Expect to pay at least €1.

9 Arte Rústica
MAP M4 ▪ Rua Augusta 193 ▪ 213 461 004

This shop is stocked with popular regional crafts, particularly hand-painted ceramics and embroidery.

Plate from Arte Rustica

10 Conserveira de Lisboa
MAP N5 ▪ Rua dos Bacalhoeiros 34 ▪ 218 864 009

This wholesaler of sardines and other tinned fish is the kind of place that makes Baixa a living museum.

Shops

1 Azevedo Rua
MAP M3 ■ Praça Dom Pedro IV 72 ■ 213 427 511

The famous hatter at the northeastern corner of Rossio has managed to stay in business for 120 years despite the vagaries of hat-wearing fashion.

2 Manuel Tavares
MAP M3 ■ Rua da Betesga 1 ■ 213 424 209

A good, tourist-oriented deli between Rossio and Praça da Figueira, where samples of wine, cheese and ham are sometimes offered for tasting before purchase.

3 Napoleão
MAP N5 ■ Rua dos Fanqueiros 70 ■ 218 872 042

This branch of the wine-shop chain offers a friendly, personalized service. There's a wide choice of table and fortified wines, as well as some spirits.

4 Santos Ofícios
MAP N4 ■ Rua da Madalena 87 ■ 218 872 031

This is the city's best shop for handicrafts and folk art, with a selection that extends well beyond the run of the mill, including some imaginative figures made from a variety of materials.

5 Retrosaria Bijou
MAP M5 ■ Rua da Conceição 91 ■ 213 425 049

Trading since 1920, this delightful haberdashery brims with beautiful buttons, ribbons, trimmings, vivid fabrics and other fine wares, including knitting yarn and an assortment of needles and thimbles.

6 Pollux
MAP M4 ■ Rua da Madalena 251 ■ 218 811 200

Located round the back of the many-floored Pollux department store, this shop sells excellent Portuguese stainless-steel cookware, knives and other serious cooking aids.

7 Discoteca Amália
MAP M4 ■ Rua do Ouro 272 ■ 213 420 939

Not a disco, but a "disc shop", which specializes in traditional Portuguese music. It is particularly renowned for its range of *fado* music, and for its merchandise commemorating famous *fado* singer Amália Rodrigues.

8 Lisbonense
MAP M4 ■ Rua Augusta 202 ■ 213 426 712

At this old-school shoe shop styles are good value and sport an inner label to remind you of Lisbon. It specializes in orthopaedic shoes.

Doll parts, Hospital de Bonecas

9 Hospital de Bonecas
MAP M3 ■ Praça da Figueira 7 ■ 213 428 574

The doll's hospital is not much bigger than a doll's house, but full of perfectly healthy dolls, as well as clothes and furniture for them. Barbie is not much in evidence. Dried herbs are also sold here.

10 Joalharia Correia
MAP M4 ■ Rua do Ouro 245–7 ■ 213 427 384

This jewellers is the place for cutting, replacing and repairing semi-precious and precious gems. The decor of the shop reflects the family's colonial African background.

See map on p68

Bars and Cafés

1 Nicola
MAP L3 ▪ Praça Dom Pedro IV 24

Rossio's premier outdoor café is well sited for people-watching. It has a venerable history and a handsome marble Art Deco interior. Downstairs is a restaurant. Coffee is cheaper at the bar and more expensive outside.

2 Pastelaria Suiça
MAP M3 ▪ Praça Dom Pedro IV 96–100

Suiça, across the square from Nicola, has a shorter history, a longer terrace and a wider selection of pastries and snacks.

Confeitaria Nacional

3 Confeitaria Nacional
MAP M3 ▪ Praça da Figueira 18

A Lisbon institution for its splendid cakes and pastries. It has a busy takeaway service and café tables inside under a mirrored ceiling.

4 A Licorista
MAP M4 ▪ Rua dos Sapateiros 218

Rustic bar and restaurant with a grand, vaulted-brick ceiling. The next-door restaurant, O Bacalhoeiro, has the same owners.

5 The British Bar
MAP L6 ▪ Rua Bernardino Costa 52

At what was once the Taverna Inglesa, haunt of Brits from local shipping firms, there is a wide selection of beers available here.

6 VIP Éden
MAP L2 ▪ Praça dos Restauradores 24

Head-spinning views of downtown Lisbon are the main draw at this café at the top of the VIP Executive Éden Aparthotel (see p117). Just ask at reception and press T for "terrace" in the elevator.

7 Café Martinho da Arcada
MAP N5 ▪ Praça do Comércio 3

This bustling, attractively tiled café serves good-value lunches at the counter. There are a few tables inside and more outside under the arcades. This is a quintessential Lisbon location.

8 Beira Gare
MAP L3 ▪ Rua 1 Dezembro 116

Best known for its *bifanas* (spicy pork sandwiches), this popular place also serves a range of seafood dishes.

9 O'Gilin's
MAP K6 ▪ Rua dos Remolares 8

Lisbon's first Irish pub is still the city's best, popular with students and expats alike. At weekends there is live music and dancing.

10 A Ginjinha
MAP M3 ▪ Largo de São Domingos 8

Ginjinha is Portuguese cherry liqueur and this tiny bar serves virtually nothing else, surviving for over 150 years on sheer single-mindedness.

The diminutive A Ginjinha

Restaurants

PRICE CATEGORIES
For a three-course meal for one with half a bottle of wine (or equivalent meal), taxes and extra charges.

€ under €20   €€ €20–€40   €€€ over €40

1 Da Vinci
MAP L2 ▪ Rua Jardim do Regedor 37 ▪ 213 461 727 ▪ €€
With plenty of outdoor seating and freshly made pizza and pasta, this is one of the best Italian restaurants in downtown Lisbon.

2 Gambrinus
MAP L2 ▪ Rua das Portas de Santo Antão 23 ▪ 213 421 466 ▪ €€€
This classic Lisbon address is as famous for its seafood dishes and "rich fish soup" as it is for its high prices and endless business lunches.

3 Martinho da Arcada
MAP M5 ▪ Praça do Comércio 3 ▪ 218 879 259 ▪ Closed Sun ▪ €€–€€€
Once a favourite with literary figures such as Fernando Pessoa, this is a great setting in which to try some traditional Portuguese food.

4 O Bacalhoeiro
MAP M4 ▪ Rua dos Sapateiros 222 ▪ 213 431 415 ▪ Closed Sun ▪ €€
This cosy restaurant is named after the Portuguese trawlers that fished cod off the coast of Newfoundland, then salted it on board.

5 Alfândega – Armazém dos Sabores
MAP N5 ▪ Rua da Alfândega 98 ▪ 218 861 683 ▪ Closed L; Sun ▪ €
Light, Mediterranean-style dishes are served in a pleasant, colourful space next to the Conceição church (see p69).

6 Cervejaria Solmar
MAP L2 ▪ Rua das Portas de Santo Antão 106 ▪ 213 230 098 ▪ €€
This beer-hall seafood restaurant has a wonderful 1950s interior.

7 Leão d'Ouro
MAP L3 ▪ Rua 1 de Dezembro 105 ▪ 213 426 195 ▪ €€
This cathedral-like restaurant is indeed a temple: to fish. Super-fresh specimens are on tempting display.

Interior of Casa do Alentejo

8 Casa do Alentejo
MAP L2 ▪ Rua das Portas de Santo Antão 58 (upstairs) ▪ 213 405 140 ▪ €€
This Neo-Moorish former palace is home to an association for people from the Alentejo region. The restaurant is open to all and serves simple Alentejan food in various memorable rooms.

9 Bonjardim Rei dos Frangos
MAP L2 ▪ Travessa de Santo Antão 14 ▪ 213 427 424 ▪ Closed Mon, Tue L ▪ €
Grilled chicken with *piri-piri* (chilli) is one of the fondest food memories many visitors take away from Portugal. This is one of the best places to sample it.

10 Varanda de Lisboa
MAP M3 ▪ Hotel Mundial, Praça Martim Moniz 2 ▪ 218 842 000 ▪ €€
Diners can enjoy great views of the Baixa from this restaurant at the top of Hotel Mundial. The traditional Portuguese food is excellent and the service is exceptional.

See map on p68

TOP 10 Chiado and Bairro Alto

Chiado is where some of Lisbon's hill neighbourhoods, steeped in history, collided with the new layout of Baixa, Pombal's reconstructed city centre. Today, both areas are old and venerated, and packed with shops, but Chiado's history and cultural institutions give its commercial activities a gilt edge. Higher up is Bairro Alto – the "high neighbourhood" – a 16th-century maze of narrow streets framed by the wider lanes and longer blocks of later construction. It may be the district of Lisbon with the highest concentration of bars, but it is also a residential area and, at its western end, a quiet neighbourhood of grand old mansions.

Tile from Igreja de São Roque

AREA MAP OF CHIADO AND BAIRRO ALTO

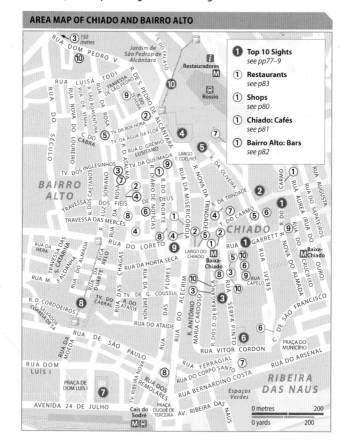

1	**Top 10 Sights** see pp77–9
1	**Restaurants** see p83
1	**Shops** see p80
1	**Chiado: Cafés** see p81
1	**Bairro Alto: Bars** see p82

1 Rua do Carmo and Rua Garrett

MAP L4

Chiado's main arteries flow at right angles to each other, meeting in front of Armazéns do Chiado, a shopping centre housed in the shell of a burned-out department store. These partly pedestrianized and sometimes steeply inclined streets are among Lisbon's most bustling. Walk up from Baixa to the top, where the café A Brasileira (see p81) awaits.

Outdoor café tables, Rua Garrett

2 Largo and Igreja do Carmo

MAP L4 ■ 10am–7pm Mon–Sat (10am–6pm winter) ■ Adm

Accessible from Baixa using the Elevador de Santa Justa (see p70), the ruins of the 14th-century Carmo church act as a memorial to the 1755 earthquake, which destroyed much of the structure. The quiet square in front of the church seems an unlikely setting for one of the most dramatic events in recent Portuguese history. It was here that army tanks threatened the barracks of the National Guard, next to the Carmo church, where Marcelo Caetano, the country's dictator, had taken refuge on 25 April 1974. His surrender ended 42 years of fascist dictatorship in Portugal.

3 Teatro Nacional de São Carlos

MAP L5 ■ Rua Serpa Pinto 9 ■ 213 253 000 ■ Box office 1–7pm Mon–Fri ■ Ticket prices vary ■ www.tnsc.pt

Lisbon's opera house, dating from 1793, is regarded as the city's first Neo-Classical building. Its grand façade – the only side of the building decorated, in keeping with post-earthquake regulations – takes its cue from Milan's La Scala, although the floorplan resembles that of Naples' San Carlo opera. The grand interior owes more to the Baroque, with its gilt wood, marble and plush. There is a café and restaurant with tables in the square (see p81).

4 Igreja e Museu de São Roque

The Jesuit church of St Roch, built in the second half of the 16th century on the edge of what would become Bairro Alto, is a monument to the wealth of religious orders and the extravagance of Dom João V – although you wouldn't know it from the outside. Inside, its chapel to St John the Baptist has been described as one of the most expensive ever made. It was assembled in Rome in the 1740s, from the most precious materials available at the time, then disassembled and shipped to Lisbon to be put back together again. The church's museum of sacred art holds an impressive collection of vestments and paintings (see p41).

Chapel of St John the Baptist, Igreja de São Roque

Calçada do Duque

5 Calçada do Duque
MAP L3

This series of steps, from Largo Trindade Coelho to the bottom of Calçada do Carmo, is a treat. Along the gradual descent are Café Buenos Aires (see p83) and a number of other restaurants. The view of the Castelo de São Jorge, foreshortened above Rossio, is perfectly framed.

6 Museu Nacional de Arte Contemporânea do Chiado (MNAC)
MAP L5 ▪ Rua Serpa Pinto 4 ▪ 10am–6pm Tue–Sun ▪ Adm (free first Sun of month) ▪ www.museuarte contemporanea.pt

Located close to the Academy of Fine Arts, this is one of the best places to view Portuguese art from the mid-19th century on. The core collection concentrates on the 1850–1950 period, but recent acquisitions and temporary shows bring things up to date.

Elevador da Bica

LISBON'S BOHEMIAN DISTRICT

Bairro Alto's reputation for loose living and drinking goes back several centuries. Even when this was a smart residential district in the 17th and 18th centuries, it had a shadier side. In the 19th century, after newspaper offices and printing shops moved in, the authorities decided to make Bairro Alto a zone of regulated prostitution. The area **(below)** has since been tidied up, but it is still at the heart of the city's nightlife.

7 Mercado da Ribeira
MAP K5 ▪ Avenida 24 de Julho ▪ 213 244 980 ▪ 10am–midnight Sun–Wed, 10am–2am Thu–Sat

Lisbon's main fish, fruit and vegetable market is a riot of fresh produce from dawn to midday. It also has a popular food hall, where a wide selection of stalls, bars and cafés offer cakes, cheeses and full meals, enjoyed at communal tables.

8 Elevador da Bica
MAP K4 ▪ Largo do Calhariz at Rua da Bica Duarte Belo ▪ 7am–9pm Mon–Sat, 9am–9pm Sun & public holidays ▪ Bus/tram ticket

Opened in 1892, this is the smallest of Lisbon's funiculars, passing through the lively neighbourhood

of Bica on its way between Largo do Calhariz and Rua de São Paulo. Like Lisbon's other funiculars, it is powered by an electric motor, which moves the cable to which both cars are attached so that they counterbalance each other and lighten the motor's load.

9 Praça Luís de Camões
MAP K4

This square, where Chiado meets Bairro Alto, is a favourite rendezvous point. It is named after the Portuguese poet laureate, whose heroic bronze, with lesser chroniclers and colleagues in stone around his feet, presides over the bright white stone oval traffic island. It used to be shaded by magnificent umbrella pines, but these have been replaced by still-puny poplars.

Praça Luís de Camões

10 Elevador da Glória
MAP K3 ■ Praça dos Restauradores at Calçada da Glória ■ 7:15am–11:55pm Mon–Thu (to 12:25am Fri), 8:45–12:25am Sat, 9:15am–11:55pm Sun & public holidays ■ Bus/tram ticket

Lisbon's best-known and now its busiest funicular links Restauradores with Bairro Alto. The second to be built, it was inaugurated in 1885. Formerly, the cars were open-top double-deckers, propelled by cog-rail and cable, with a water counterweight. Later on, steam power was used, but in 1915 the Glória went electric.

CHIADO TO BAIRRO ALTO AND THE BICA

Lost In — *La Paparrucha*
Elevador da Glória
Rua da Rosa — *Igreja de São Roque*
Calçada do Duque
Solar do Vinho do Porto — *Cervejaria Trindade*
Carmo
Elevador da Bica — *Vertigo*
Miradouro de Santa Catarina
O'Gilins — *The British Bar*
Cais do Sodré

▶ MORNING

Begin by the **Carmo** ruins. If you're coming from Baixa, take the Elevador de Santa Justa. Crossing to the bottom left-hand corner of the square, take Travessa do Carmo, stopping for coffee at **Vertigo** *(see p81)*. Cross Largo Rafael Bordalo Pinheiro to Rua da Trindade and then Rua Nova da Trindade, on which turn right. Passing the famous **Cervejaria Trindade** on the right, you soon reach the top of **Calçada do Duque**. Straight ahead is **Igreja de São Roque**. Past the church, the street leads to the top of the **Elevador da Glória** on your right, and the **Solar do Vinho do Porto** on your left. For lunch, carry on up the street and try **Lost In** at no. 56d, or the steak house **La Paparrucha** at no.18/20.

AFTERNOON

After lunch, stroll at your leisure in Bairro Alto, entering via **Rua da Rosa** on the other side of Rua Dom Pedro V. Keep track of Rua da Rosa, which will take you out of the area on the other side. Here, across the street, is the top of the **Elevador da Bica**. Ride it down to Rua de São Paulo and then head left towards Cais do Sodré, taking a drink at **O'Gilin's** or **The British Bar** *(see p74)*. Otherwise, you can walk halfway up the steep hill again and turn left into one of the narrow streets to reach **Miradouro de Santa Catarina** *(see p42)* and afternoon refreshments in the open air.

See map on p76 ←

Shops

1 Luvaria Ulisses
MAP L4 ■ Rua do Carmo 87A
This small gem of a shop is the only one in Portugal selling just gloves. Hand sewn, they have a lifetime guarantee covering repairs.

2 Leitão & Irmão
MAP L4 ■ Largo do Chiado 16
Jewellery and silverware from a company that was appointed crown jewellers in 1875. Their pieces are held in museums and private collections the world over, and sold at a shop in Lisbon's Ritz hotel.

Leitão & Irmão
"Viana Heart"
pendant

3 Embaixada
MAP J2 ■ Praça do Príncipe Real 26
This trendy shopping centre, with 18 boutique-style establishments, sells a range of items, such as eco-friendly cosmetics, handcrafted jewellery and fine clothing. Open until midnight.

4 A Carioca
MAP L4 ■ Rua da Misericórdia 9
Coffee beans from Africa, Asia and South America are roasted on the premises and sold either freshly ground or whole at this specialist shop. Tea and hot chocolate are also available; try the chocolate sourced from São Tomé.

5 Vista Alegre
MAP L4 ■ Largo do Chiado 20–21
The work of Portugal's premier porcelain maker is wide-ranging: from modern to traditional designs, and from restrained tableware to exuberant decorative pieces.

6 A Vida Portuguesa
MAP L4 ■ Rua Anchieta 11
This attractive shop in the heart of the Chiado sells the best of Portuguese jewellery, ceramics and toys.

7 Storytailors
MAP L5 ■ Calçada do Ferragial 8 ■ Closed Sun & Mon
Showcasing the talents of young designers João Branco and Luís Sanchez, this store specializes in glamorous, fairy-tale themed dresses and bridal gowns.

8 El Dorado
MAP K4 ■ Rua do Norte 23
This retro fashion boutique stocks seriously collectable Victorian lace gowns, 1960s psychedelic tunics, motorbike jackets and other vintage apparel.

9 Armazéns do Chiado
MAP L4 ■ Rua do Carmo 2
In the restored shell of what was Lisbon's poshest department store (destroyed by fire in 1988) is the city's most central shopping centre. The larger retailers here include FNAC.

10 Livraria Bertrand
MAP L4 ■ Rua Garrett 73
The Bertrand chain has branches all over the city; this one is Lisbon's oldest bookshop, stocking a wide selection of English-language titles in its warren of rooms.

Coffee beans, A Carioca

Chiado: Cafés

1 A Brasileira
MAP L4 ▪ Rua Garrett 120

The city's most famous café is an Art Nouveau tunnel of florid stuccowork, mirrors and paintings from its 1920s heyday. The tables outside, where a bronze statue of poet Fernando Pessoa lingers today, are among Lisbon's most coveted.

Coffee at the counter, A Brasileira

2 Bénard
MAP L4 ▪ Rua Garrett 104

"The other café" is, in fact, a tearoom serving cakes and pastries that some consider superior to those of its neighbour. Its outdoor tables serve as a welcome extension to A Brasileira's often crowded terrace.

3 No Chiado
MAP L5 ▪ Largo do Picadeiro 12

This tranquil café is just a block from the bustle of Rua Garrett, but feels a whole world away. Al fresco tables, internet access and light meals are all available.

4 Royale
MAP L4 ▪ Largo Rafael Bordalo Pinheiro 29

Organic light lunches, snacks and cakes are served in this elegant café, which has a small interior courtyard. The service is excellent.

5 Leitaria Académica
MAP L4 ▪ Largo do Carmo 1

This venerable milk bar is named after Lisbon's first university. Its outdoor tables in peaceful Largo do Carmo are popular. Hearty meals are also served.

6 Sacramento
MAP L4 ▪ Calçada do Sacramento 40

This place is a labyrinth on different levels, all pleasantly cool, with whitewashed walls and bare-brick arches. The café overlooks the street; there is also a restaurant and a club.

7 Vertigo
MAP L4 ▪ Travessa do Carmo 4

A warm ambience permeates this café, whose heavy-framed mirrors and stained wood give it something of an old-world feel. Its informal service and organic snacks are, however, bang up to date.

8 Cafetaria de São Carlos
MAP L5 ▪ Largo São Carlos 23

Next to the São Carlos opera house (see p77) is a square that was once used as a car park. Now one corner of it is a permanent terrace attached to the opera's restaurant and café – a peaceful Chiado stopping point.

9 Kaffeehaus
MAP L5 ▪ Rua Anchieta 3

This busy café-bar brings a delightful dash of Vienna to the Portuguese capital. Grab an outside table in the sun and relax with a coffee and tasty apple strudel.

10 Café no Chiado
MAP L5 ▪ Largo do Picadeiro 10

A popular meeting place for writers, musicians and artists, this colourful café has shelves stacked with books and periodicals. It serves a range of delicious light meals and snacks. There is a beautiful outdoor terrace with wonderful views.

See map on p76

Bairro Alto: Bars

1 Artis
MAP K4 ■ Rua Diário de Notícias 95

Artis is one of Bairro Alto's most lived-in bars. It's a great place for those who like low lights, jazz and the buzz of conversation.

2 Solar do Vinho do Porto
MAP K3 ■ Rua de São Pedro de Alcântara 45

Located in an 18th-century building, this cool, lounge-like bar has been going for many years. It boasts an impressive list of wines that can be ordered by the glass or bottle.

3 Portas Largas
MAP K3 ■ Rua da Atalaia 105

This is the Bairro Alto in a nutshell. "Wide Doors", as it is called, is a rustic tavern-turned-bar, whose party spills out onto the street. The crowd is young, friendly and laid-back.

4 Capela
MAP K4 ■ Rua da Atalaia 45

The decor of this DJ bar combines sparseness with extravagance. The deep yet narrow space can get extremely crowded – but always with an interesting mix of people.

5 Bibo Bar
MAP K3 ■ Travessa da Água da Flor 43

A lounge bar by day and live music venue by night, Bibo Bar also hosts photography exhibitions and stand-up comedy. Wi-Fi is available.

6 Clube da Esquina
MAP K4 ■ Rua da Barroca 30

The "Corner Club" is a chatty, crowded, yet relaxed place whose well-lit interior, with exposed wooden beams, has framed many a good start to a Bairro Alto night. Excellent selection of cocktails.

7 BA Wine Bar
MAP K3 ■ Rua da Rosa 107

This small, atmospheric wine bar, in the heart of the Bairro Alto, serves around 200 different wines by the glass, including a bottle of Madeira dating back to 1883. The bar also serves a variety of hams and cheeses.

8 Pensão Amor
MAP K5 ■ Rua do Alecrim 19

Eclectic music adds to the appeal of this sumptuously decorated, Burlesque-themed bar.

9 Aché Cohiba
MAP K4 ■ Rua do Norte 121

Lisbon's liveliest Cuban bar promises a real taste of Havana, with frenzied DJ sessions and deadly cocktails.

10 Pavilhão Chinês
MAP K2 ■ Rua Dom Pedro V 89

One of the oldest bars in Bairro Alto, this place is something completely different. Every spare inch of wall space is covered with a bizarre collection of paintings, porcelain, Airfix models, dolls and hats.

Quirky interior of Pavilhão Chinês

Restaurants

1 Tavares

Founded in 1784, Lisbon's oldest restaurant has an ornate Edwardian interior with gilded wood, stucco and red plush. The Portuguese menu has been revived by local chef Hélder Martins *(see p52)*.

The modern interior at Pap'Açorda

2 Pap'Açorda

MAP K4 ■ Rua da Atalaia 57–9 ■ 213 464 811 ■ Closed L; Sun ■ €€€

Açorda is a rustic soup dish of the Alentejo region, here successfully made into a modern and glamorous meal. The rest of the menu also mixes tradition with a dash of innovation.

3 Belcanto

MAP L5 ■ Largo de Sao Carlos 10 ■ 213 420 607 ■ Closed Sun, Mon ■ €€€

A long-established Chiado restaurant with two Michelin stars and a charmingly traditional ambience. The modern menu is sourced from local, seasonal produce.

4 Antigo 1 de Maio

MAP K4 ■ Rua da Atalaia 8 ■ 213 426 840 ■ Closed Sat L, Sun ■ €€

This family-run eatery serves traditional Portuguese fare such as *carne do porco à alentejana* (pork with clams in garlic and olive oil).

5 Largo

MAP L5 ■ Rua Serpa Pinto 10a ■ 213 477 225 ■ €€€

A gastronomic landmark, this fashionable contemporary restaurant has a striking setting: the cloisters of the former Igreja dos Mártires.

6 Tágide

MAP L5 ■ Largo da Academia Nacional de Belas Artes 18–20 ■ 213 404 010 ■ Closed Sun ■ €€€

This elegant restaurant serves delicious French-influenced Portuguese cuisine.

7 Café Buenos Aires

MAP L3 ■ Calçada Escadinhas do Duque 31B ■ 213 420 739 ■ €€

On the steps between Bairro Alto and Rossio, this cozy Argentinian-inspired place has tables outside and a menu that is not all meat.

8 Adega das Mercês

MAP K4 ■ Travessa das Mercês 2 ■ 213 424 492 ■ Closed Sun ■ €

Classic Bairro Alto restaurant specializing in grilled fish and meat. The portions are huge.

Dessert at 100 Maneiras

9 100 Maneiras

MAP K3 ■ Rua do Teixeira 35 ■ 210 990 475 ■ Closed L daily ■ €€€

Quality and creativity characterize the cuisine at this low-key place. The tasting menu is excellent.

10 Casanostra

MAP K4 ■ Travessa do Poço da Cidade 60 ■ 213 425 931 ■ Closed Sat L ■ €€

One of Lisbon's first Italian restaurants remains one of its best, serving more than just good pasta.

See map on p76

🔟 West Lisbon

West Lisbon comprises a series of hills on either side of the Alcântara Valley, now filled with traffic rather than water. The city's former aqueduct spans the valley, disappearing into the Monsanto Park on Lisbon's highest hill. Opposite, the residential districts of Campo de Ourique, Estrela and Lapa descend in steep steps south towards the river. The waterfront from the Alcântara docks to Belém is straight and accessible, with the 25 de Abril bridge arching overhead.

Puppet in the Casa Fernando Pessoa

The expansive Jardim Botânico

① Jardim Botânico
MAP J1–2 ■ Rua da Escola Politécnica 54 ■ 213 921 800 ■ Garden 9am–8pm (6pm in winter) ■ Adm (free until 2pm Sun)

Central Lisbon's sloping botanic garden was laid out in the second half of the 19th century, replacing Ajuda as the main showcase for

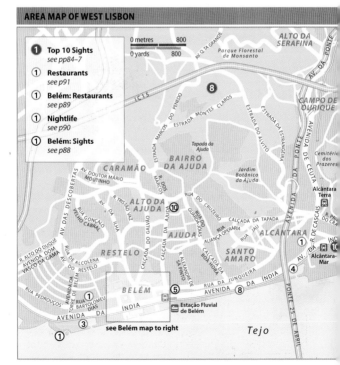

AREA MAP OF WEST LISBON

① Top 10 Sights
see pp84–7

① Restaurants
see p91

① Belém: Restaurants
see p89

① Nightlife
see p90

① Belém: Sights
see p88

see Belém map to right

exotic flora, due to its more central location. The buildings at the top of the garden now house various museums, including the child-friendly Science Museum *(see p49)*.

2 Casa Fernando Pessoa
MAP E4 ■ Rua Coelho da Rocha 16–18 ■ 213 913 270 ■ 10am–6pm Mon–Sat ■ Adm

Portugal's great modernist poet Fernando Pessoa lived in this building from 1920 until his death in 1935. Later acquired and comprehensively redesigned by the city council, in 1993 it opened as a museum dedicated to Pessoa and to poetry. It houses the poet's personal library, books about him, and a collection of Portuguese and foreign poetry. There is also a space for temporary exhibitions and events, some of Pessoa's furniture, and the poet's room, which is "recreated" at irregular intervals by invited artists. There's a restaurant in the small, modernist-style back garden.

Casa Fernando Pessoa

3 Belém
Now part of a larger city, rather than the distant suburb it was in the pre-motorized era, Lisbon's westernmost district nonetheless retains pleasant contrasts with the city centre. Refreshing river breezes and a cluster of some of Lisbon's main sights *(see p88)* contribute to Belém's appeal.

4 Estrela
MAP E4 ■ Praça da Estrela

The area between Campo de Ourique and Lapa takes its name from the Basílica da Estrela *(see p40)*, opposite the entrance to central Lisbon's most agreeable park, Jardim da Estrela. It is a distinctly British part of Lisbon, with the British embassy and English Cemetery (where Henry Fielding is buried) close by.

5 Assembleia da República
MAP F4 ■ Largo das Cortes ■ 213 919 625 ■ Guided tours: 3–4:30pm & 4–5:30pm on last Sat of month

This building has been the seat of the Portuguese parliament since 1833, when the Benedictine monks of the Convento de São Bento da Saúde were evicted – a year before the dissolution of religious orders. The vast monastery was adapted in fits and starts; today's formal Neo-Classical building was designed at the end of the 19th century.

6 Museu da Marioneta

MAP F5 ▪ Rua da Esperança 146 (Convento das Bernardas) ▪ 213 942 810 ▪ 10am–1pm, 2–6pm Tue–Sun ▪ Adm

Lisbon's Puppet Museum has a collection of over 400 puppets from all over the world, as well as scenery, props and machinery for puppet shows. It is housed in a former convent, which it shares with housing and the gourmet restaurant A Travessa (see p52). The museum also puts on shows and has puppet-making workshops for school groups.

Mask from the Museu da Marioneta

7 Museu Nacional de Arte Antiga

Portugal's national museum (see pp18–19) holds some of the country's greatest artistic treasures, as well as foreign masterpieces such as Bosch's *The Temptations of St Anthony* – a painting about the Egyptian St Anthony, founder of Christian monasticism, rather than St Anthony of Padua, Lisbon's most popular patron saint.

Detail, *The Temptations of St Anthony*

A GOLDEN GATE FOR EUROPE

By the time the steel suspension bridge (**above**) was built across the Tejo in 1962–6, bridges had been proposed at various sites for nearly a century. Similar in design to San Francisco's Golden Gate bridge, Ponte Salazar (as it was originally called) is just over 1 km (about half a mile) long, which made it Europe's longest bridge when it opened in 1966. Its two towers are just under 200 m (650 ft) tall. Renamed Ponte 25 de Abril for the date of the Carnation Revolution in 1974, it has been adapted to increasing traffic over the years by squeezing in extra lanes and adding a railway crossing underneath. The 1998 opening of the Vasco da Gama bridge has relieved the bridge's notorious traffic jams.

8 Monsanto

MAP D2

Monsanto is Lisbon's largest wooded area and its highest hill. It is the best place to go around central Lisbon for the smell of pine trees, a fresh breeze, and a walk with soil underfoot. Fitness equipment has been installed and paths have been laid out for walking, as well as cycling. There are a number of fenced-off recreational areas, including children's parks (see p48), tennis courts, a shooting range, a camp site and a rugby pitch. It's an area well worth exploring – but only during daylight hours.

9 Aqueduto das Águas Livres

MAP F3 ▪ 218 100 215

Lisbon's long-legged aqueduct was commissioned by Dom João V in the early 18th century, and aimed to increase the city's supply of drinking water by drawing in fresh water from springs at the nearby parish of Caneças. Funded by a sales tax on products such as olive oil, meat and wine, construction on the aqueduct started in 1731, and by 1748 it was beginning to bring water into the city. Officially completed in 1799, the aqueduct carried water across 58 km (36 miles) of ducting. The system was only taken out of service in 1967. The Museu da Água organizes walks across the aqueduct.

The 18th-century arches of the Aqueduto das Águas Livres

⑩ Museu do Oriente

MAP D5 ■ Avenida Brasília, Doca de Alcântara (Norte) ■ 213 585 200 ■ 10am–6pm Tue–Sun (10pm Fri) ■ Adm (free 6–10pm Fri)

Located in an old dockside building, this fascinating museum celebrates Portugal's links with the Far East across the ages. Highlights include a magnificent collection of 17th- and 18th-century Chinese and Japanese folding screens, as well as rare pieces of Ming porcelain and Namban art. Perhaps the most popular attraction is the Kwok On Collection, which consists of costumes, musical instruments, puppets and etchings from Japan, Korea, Myanmar (Burma), Cambodia and Iran.

A WALK THROUGH WEST LISBON

▶ MORNING

Begin by catching the 28 tram to its terminus at **Prazeres**. Visit the cemetery of the same name, then stroll along Rua Saraiva de Carvalho past the large **Santo Condestável** church, with its attractive stained-glass windows. Drop into **Campo de Ourique** market *(see p54)* and pick up some fresh fruit, or just whet your appetite for lunch. Then head right along Rua Coelho da Rocha and visit **Casa Fernando Pessoa**. Lunch here, or at the cozy **Tasca da Esquina** *(see p91)*, in Rua Domingos Sequeira.

AFTERNOON

After lunch, walk all the way down Rua Coelho da Rocha, turn right into Rua da Estrela, and proceed downhill to one of the corner entrances of **Jardim da Estrela**, where you can absorb the peace of the park. When you're ready, head for the main entrance and you'll see the **Basílica de Estrela** across the square. After a visit, make your way through Lapa via Rua João de Deus, which enters it on the left of the basilica. Follow the tram tracks round and then down Rua de São Domingos – veer off to left or right for extended Lapa views. Return to Rua de São Domingos and continue until you reach steps leading down to Rua das Janelas Verdes and the **Museu Nacional de Arte Antiga (MNAA)** *(see pp18–19)*.

See map on pp84–5

Belém: Sights

View from the Torre de Belém

1 Torre de Belém
For many, this defensive tower is the masterpiece of the Manueline style (see pp22–3).

2 Palácio de Belém
MAP B6 ▪ Praça Afonso de Albuquerque ▪ 213 614 660 ▪ Palace and gardens: 10:30am–4:30pm Sat (guided visit only); Museum: 10am–6pm Tue–Fri, 10am–1pm & 2–6pm Sat & Sun ▪ Adm

This 16th-century palace, altered by Dom João V, is the working residence of Portugal's president. It houses the Museu da Presidência da República.

3 Mosteiro dos Jerónimos
Portugal's greatest national monument is emblematic of the country's Manueline style. Dom Manuel I built the monastery and abbey in the early 16th century, in thanks for Portugal's voyages of maritime discovery (see pp14–15).

4 Museu de Arqueologia
MAP A6 ▪ Praça do Império ▪ 213 620 000 ▪ 10am–6pm Tue–Sun ▪ Adm (free first Sun of month)

Housed in the west wing of the Mosteiro dos Jerónimos, this museum exhibits archaeological finds from the Iron Age onwards.

5 Museu Nacional dos Coches
The museum of historic coaches (see p38) is in the former riding school of the Palácio de Belém, though most of the collection is housed in a building on Praça Afonso de Albuquerque.

6 Museu Coleção Berardo
This prestigious collection of modern art includes works by Picasso and Andy Warhol (see p56).

7 Padrão dos Descobrimentos
MAP B6 ▪ Avenida de Brasília ▪ 213 031 950 ▪ Mar–Sep: 10am–7pm daily; Oct–Feb: 10am–6pm Tue–Sun ▪ Adm

Created in 1960 for the 500th anniversary of the death of Henry the Navigator (see p37), this monument takes the form of the prow of a ship.

8 Museu de Marinha
MAP A6 ▪ Praça do Império ▪ 213 620 019 ▪ 10am–5pm (6pm in summer) Tue–Sun ▪ Adm (free first Sun of month)

Astrolabe, Museu de Marinha

The naval museum in the west wing of the Mosteiro dos Jerónimos covers the history of shipbuilding and navigation.

9 Jardim Botânico Tropical
MAP B5–6 ▪ Largo dos Jerónimos ▪ 213 609 665 ▪ Feb, Mar & Oct: 10am–6pm; Apr & Sep: 10am–7pm; May–Aug: 10am–8pm; Nov–Jan: 10am–5pm ▪ Adm

This garden of tropical trees and plants – the research centre of the Institute for Tropical Sciences – is an oasis in the tourist bustle of Belém.

10 Palácio da Ajuda
MAP B5 ▪ Largo da Ajuda ▪ 213 620 264 ▪ 10am–5:30pm Thu–Tue ▪ Adm

The Neo-Classical Ajuda palace was left unfinished in 1807 when the royal family was forced into exile in Brazil.

Belém: Restaurants

PRICE CATEGORIES
For a three-course meal for one with half a bottle of wine (or equivalent meal), taxes and extra charges.

€ under €20 €€ €20–€40 €€€ over €40

1 Nunes
MAP A6 ■ Rua Bartolomeu Dias 112 ■ 213 019 899 ■ Closed Mon ■ €€
Located close to Lisbon's top tourist attractions, Nunes is renowned for its fresh seafood.

2 Solar do Embaixador
MAP B6 ■ Rua do Embaixador 210 ■ 213 625 111 ■ €
Tasty Brazilian specialities share the menu with more traditional Portuguese fare at this jolly restaurant in a Belém backstreet.

3 Vela Latina
MAP A6 ■ Doca do Bom Sucesso ■ 213 017 118 ■ Closed Sun ■ €€
Overlooking the Bom Sucesso dock, this place specializes in creative fish and seafood dishes. Try the *filetes de pescada* (hake fillets).

4 Nosolo Itália
MAP B6 ■ Avenida de Brasília 202 ■ 213 015 969 ■ €€
Fine river views and a wide choice (for vegetarians, too) of pastas, pizzas and salads are on offer here.

5 Cais de Belém
MAP B6 ■ Rua Vieira Portuense 64 ■ 213 621 537 ■ Closed Tue D, Wed ■ €€
Located next to the Jardim de Belém, the traditional Cais de Belém does a reliable *arroz de peixe com gambas* (fish rice with prawns).

6 Belém 2 a 8
MAP B6 ■ Rua de Belém 2 ■ 213 639 055 ■ Closed Mon ■ €€
Vegetarians can enjoy Portuguese cuisine at this brightly decorated place next to the president's palace.

7 Este Oeste
MAP A6 ■ Centro Cultural de Belém, Praça do Império ■ 215 904 358 ■ €€
An open-plan restaurant with magnificent river views, Este Oeste specializes in Italian and Japanese cuisine, with dishes such as wood-baked pizza and freshly made sushi.

8 Café In
MAP C6 ■ Avenida de Brasília, Pavilhão Nascente 311 ■ 213 626 248 ■ €€
With a popular terrace, a groovy retro bar and a slightly more formal restaurant, this low building on the riverside is busy all day. Grilled fish and seafood dominate the menu.

9 Enoteca de Belém
MAP B6 ■ Travessa de Marta Pinto 10–12 ■ 213 631 511 ■ €€
This delightful little wine bar has an outstanding range of Portuguese wines as well as an excellent selection of delicious tapas-style tasting plates, such as grilled octopus and duck risotto.

Enoteca de Belém

10 Os Jerónimos
MAP B6 ■ Rua de Belém 74 ■ 213 638 423 ■ Closed Sat ■ €
This simple bar-restaurant provides a serious take on traditional Portuguese food. Portions are large.

See map on pp84–5

Nightlife

Laid-back club and venue Bar Lounge

nightspot on Lisbon's quayside. On-site restaurants and weekly themed parties create a vibrant atmosphere, but beware of hidden fees (see p50).

6 Main
One of the largest and liveliest clubs in Lisbon, Main caters to a varied clientele. It is divided into three distinct areas, and also offers a Portuguese restaurant (see p50).

1 Bar Lounge
This friendly and relaxed venue plays a mix of indie and electronic pop and rock music, with regular live music sessions (see p50).

2 Trumps
MAP F4 ■ Rua da Imprensa Nacional 104B
A mainstay of Lisbon's gay scene, this mixed club, spread over two levels, has several bar areas, a dance floor and a snooker room.

3 Finalmente
MAP F4 ■ Rua da Palmeira 38
Another fixture on the Lisbon gay scene, Finalmente has a tiny dance floor and notorious drag shows. The party tends to get going late, but it can get very lively as the night draws on.

4 Foxtrot
MAP F4 ■ Travessa de Santa Teresa 28
With a rambling series of rooms, a courtyard, pool tables and kitschy decor, this old-style bar has become a quintessential Lisbon hang-out.

5 K Urban Beach
Celebrities and well-heeled locals come together in this stylish

7 Europa Sunrise
Late-night partying is the theme here, with a convivial, anything-goes atmosphere. The music is usually a combination of drum and bass and trance. Entry is free some nights (see p50).

8 Station
A fashionable Lisbon night-spot with a prime riverside location, Station plays funk and soul on Thursdays and techno on Saturdays. Its ground-floor restaurant serves an Asian-inspired menu (see p50).

9 Hard Rock Café
MAP L2 ■ Avenida da Liberdade 2
This famous music-themed restaurant is well-located and houses an array of items owned by iconic rock stars, such as U2, Sir Elton John and The Eagles. The restaurant specializes in burgers and smoked ribs.

10 A Velha Senhora
MAP K6 ■ Rua Nova do Carvalho 38
Located on Lisbon's famous Pink Street in Cais do Sodré, A Velha Senhora (The Old Lady) organizes burlesque shows and an assortment of themed party nights.

Restaurants

PRICE CATEGORIES

For a three-course meal for one with half a bottle of wine (or equivalent meal), taxes and extra charges.

€ under €20 €€ €20–€40 €€€ over €40

1 Espaço Lisboa

The exquisite food at this renowned restaurant (see p52) is matched by its grand surroundings, which include a small coffee museum.

2 Kais/Adega do Kais

MAP E5 ■ Rua do Cintura do Porto de Lisboa, Cais da Viscondessa ■ 213 932 930 ■ Closed L; Sun, Mon ■ €€€

Housed in a former engine shed, Kais offers a modern Portuguese menu. Adega do Kais, in the basement, is a traditional *rodízio* (rotisserie), serving a range of dishes for a fixed price.

3 A Confraria

MAP E5 ■ York House Hotel, Rua das Janelas Verdes 32 ■ 213 962 435 ■ Closed Mon L, Tue L ■ €€

Located close to the Museu Nacional de Arte Antiga, this restaurant offers the option of dining al fresco or within its 17th-century walls. It has an excellent wine list and a menu that changes seasonally.

Catch of the day, Doca Piexe

4 Doca Piexe

MAP D5 ■ Doca de Santo Amaro, Armazém 14 ■ 213 973 565 ■ €€

Enjoy fresh seafood, such as cod with clams, while sitting outside at one of Lisbon's prime riverside locations.

5 Clube de Jornalistas

MAP E4 ■ Rua das Trinas 129 ■ 213 977 138 ■ Closed Sun ■ €€

This attractive restaurant with an inner courtyard serves top-notch contemporary international food.

6 Tasca da Esquina

MAP E4 ■ Rua Domingos Sequeira 41c ■ 210 993 939 ■ €€

Enjoy fried skate or tuna with sweet potato at this modern Lapa eatery.

7 Terra

MAP F4 ■ Rua da Palmeira 15 ■ 213 421 407 ■ Closed Mon ■ €€

This lovely vegetarian restaurant serves delicious vegetable and meat-substitute dishes.

Atmospheric dining at A Travessa

8 A Travessa

Set in a convent building, this is one of Lisbon's most characterful restaurants in terms both of location and food (see p52).

9 O Mercado

MAP D5 ■ Mercado Rosa Agulhas, Rua Leão de Oliveira ■ 213 649 113 ■ €€

What better place for a restaurant than a market building? O Mercado serves super-fresh local dishes.

10 Noobai Café

MAP J5 ■ Miradouro do Adamastor, Rua Santa Catarina ■ 213 465 014 ■ €

Enjoy river views while snacking on wholesome soups, healthy salads and light tapas. After dark, a DJ spins chill-out music.

See map on pp84–5

🔟 Avenida and North Lisbon

Avenida da Liberdade extends northwards from Restauradores at a slight incline. It ends at the roundabout named after the Marquis of Pombal, who became Lisbon's *de facto* head of government after the 1755 earthquake. He stands at the centre of the swirl of traffic, flanked by a lion, surveying the city centre he created. If you continue up to the top of Parque Eduardo VII and look to your right, Lisbon's early 20th-century northern extensions stretch out before you. Closer at hand is the esteemed Gulbenkian museum; further afield, the 21st-century vistas of Parque das Nações.

Fan, Casa-Museu Fundação Medeiros e Almeida

1 Museu Calouste Gulbenkian

Founded on the private collections and fortune of Armenian exile Calouste Gulbenkian, this museum (*see pp30–31*) is one of Lisbon's most satisfying sights. Inaugurated in 1969, it was purpose-built to display the wealthy oil magnate's bequest to the nation. It contains one of the most impressive collections of fine and decorative art in Europe.

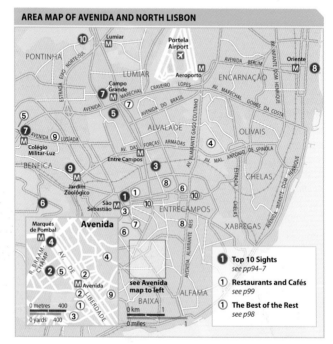

AREA MAP OF AVENIDA AND NORTH LISBON

1 Top 10 Sights
see pp94–7

1 Restaurants and Cafés
see p99

1 The Best of the Rest
see p98

Previous pages *Palácio Nacional da Pena, Sintra*

A Drawing Room in Casa-Museu Fundação Medeiros e Almeida

② Casa-Museu Fundação Medeiros e Almeida

MAP F3 ▪ Rua Rosa Araújo 41
▪ 213 547 892 ▪ www.casa-museu
medeirosealmeida.pt ▪ 1–5:30pm
Mon–Fri, 10am–5:30pm Sat ▪ Adm,
free Sat 10am–1pm.

This treasure trove of a museum was the home of businessman and private collector António Medeiros e Almeida, who died in 1986. His collection of some 2,000 objects is astonishing: there are 25 rooms featuring French and Flemish tapestries, English silver, ornate furniture, priceless paintings and Chinese porcelain. Some of the most valuable items include bronze wall fountains from the Palace of Versailles, a silver dinner service that once belonged to Napoleon and a 17th-century clock made for Queen Catherine of Bragança.

③ Campo Pequeno

MAP F1 ▪ 217 998 450
▪ Bullfights traditionally on Thu,
May–Sep ▪ Adm for events varies

One of Lisbon's most striking buildings, this bullring is a delightful Arabic-Oriental pastiche from 1892, with onion cupolas and keyhole windows. It stands on a spot where bullfights (see p96) have been held since the first half of the 18th century, when this area was part of a vast expanse of country estates. Several years of restoration have resulted in a modern leisure and shopping complex to accompany the bullring.

④ Marquês de Pombal Rotunda and Parque Eduardo VII

MAP F2–3

The roundabout where Pombal and his lion pose was the northern limit of the city he conceived. The orderly park behind him was first laid out in the late 19th century as a green extension of Avenida da Liberdade, replacing the pedestrian Passeio Público that the Avenida had usurped. In 1903, Parque da Liberdade was renamed in honour of the visiting English King Edward VII. It is really more of a steeply sloping promenade than a park. For proper greenery, seek out the Estufa Fria and Estufa Quente greenhouses along the park's northwestern edge. A walk to the top is rewarded with good views, the Linha d'Água café and Eleven restaurant (see p53).

Parque Eduardo VII and the Marquês de Pombal Rotunda

5 Museu de Lisboa

MAP C1 ■ Campo Grande 245 ■ 217 513 200 ■ 10am–6pm Tue–Sun

The museum is housed in the 18th-century Palácio Pimenta, at the top of Campo Grande. The palace itself is worth seeing, particularly for the unusual kitchen tiles depicting animal carcasses hung to tenderize. The permanent exhibition traces Lisbon's development from the earliest settlements along the Tejo. Perhaps the most evocative display is the large 3-D model of Lisbon as it is believed to have looked before the earthquake in 1755.

Tile in the Museu de Lisboa

RIDING AGAINST THE BULL

Portuguese bullfighting is always introduced with the qualification that the bull isn't killed. This attempt to appease opponents of bullfighting is misleading: in fact, the bull is unceremoniously slaughtered after the fight – a rather academic distinction. The most interesting difference compared with Spanish bullfighting – both forms successively wound the animal in order to make the finale possible – is that a rider on an unprotected horse (the bull's horns are wrapped) performs an equestrian ballet with the bull, while sticking short spears in between its shoulder blades to make its head hang lower. The finale is then performed by a group of intrepid *forcados* on foot, who charge the bull in single file, throwing themselves between its horns and over one side in order to topple it and hold it fast.

6 Palácio dos Marqueses da Fronteira

MAP B2 ■ Largo de São Domingos de Benfica 1 ■ 217 782 023 ■ Guided tours Mon–Sat; Jun–Sep: 10:30am, 11am, 11:30am, noon; Oct–May: 11am, noon ■ Adm

A 17th-century former hunting pavilion, expanded after the 1755 earthquake, this manor house and its gardens are really rewarding sights. The formal gardens are full of statues and tiled panels, from busts of Portuguese kings to allegorical representations of the seasons and the zodiac. Highlights inside the palace include the Battle Room, featuring depictions of battles during the War of Restoration against Spain – in which the first Marquis da Fronteira fought. Fronteira Palace is still owned and lived in by the 12th Marquis, who collects contemporary art and sometimes stages exhibitions.

Tilework, Palácio dos Marqueses da Fronteira

7 Football Stadiums
MAP B1 ■ Benfica: Rua
Fernando da Fonseca; 707 200 100
■ **Sporting:** Avenida General Norton
de Matos; 217 516 444 ■ Match
tickets from €20

Lisbon's two main football teams,
Benfica and Sporting, both rebuilt
their stadiums for the Euro 2004
championships, held in Portugal.
Sporting's green and yellow Estádio
José Alvalade is on the northern city
limits. A short distance west is
Benfica's red Estádio da Luz. Both
teams have interesting museums and
offer guided tours of the stadiums.

Parque das Nações waterfront

8 Parque das Nações
The former Expo 98 site is
now a business and leisure area,
with exhibition spaces, events
venues and a variety of sights
(see pp20–21).

9 Jardim Zoológico
Lisbon's Zoo is a sprightly
centenarian, incorporating a small
amusement park and the usual
selection of animals (see p48).

10 Parque do Monteiro-Mor
MAP B1 ■ Largo Júlio de
Castilho ■ 217 567 620 ■ Open 10am–
6pm Wed–Sun, 2–6pm Tue ■ Adm
(covers park and both museums)

Despite its unpromising location next
to one of the major northern exits
from Lisbon, this lovely Italianate
park is one of the city's best oases.
With its palace – now housing two
moderately interesting museums
devoted to Theatre and Costume –
it is a reminder of what Lisbon's
hinterland was once like.

TO THE GULBENKIAN AND BEYOND

▶ **MORNING**

Begin at the **Pombal Roundabout**.
An underpass leads to the statue,
where you can study its various
representations of tidal waves,
destruction, and the enlightened
despot's many reforms. Cross
back to the bottom of **Parque
Eduardo VII** and set out for the
summit; be aware that the walk
is unshaded and it gets very hot
in summer. If you need a break,
dive into the cool of the **Estufa
Fria** and **Quente greenhouses**.
At the top, ponder the symbolism
of João Cutileiro's **Monument to
25 April** and its contrast with Keil
do Amaral's **twin columns**. Then
climb the last bit of the hill to
Linha d'Água; have lunch here,
or enjoy a lavish gourmet meal
at the adjacent **Eleven**.

AFTERNOON

After lunch, continue past **El
Corte Inglés** and on to the side
entrance of the **Museu Calouste
Gulbenkian**, at the north end of
Avenida António Augusto de
Aguiar. Expect to spend most of
the afternoon in the museum – or
give it a quick browse and come
back later. Stroll through the park
and exit on Rua Marquês de Sá
Bandeira, then take Avenida
Miguel Bombarda for a taste of
the **Avenidas Novas**. Turn left
onto Avenida da República and
walk a few blocks north to **Campo
Pequeno** with its Neo-Moorish
bullring. Stop for a drink in the
surrounding park before a spot
of window-shopping.

See map on p94

The Best of the Rest

1 Hot Clube
MAP K1 ▪ Praça da Alegria 48

Lisbon's oldest jazz club is indifferent to shifting fashions. Inside this small basement club, the gap between artists and audience evaporates.

2 Avenida Designer Shops
MAP F3 ▪ Avenida da Liberdade

The former Passeio Público (Public Promenade) still hasn't recovered from the introduction of vehicles over a century ago. However, the appearance of international designer shops shows that Lisbon's main avenue has regained some of its pedigree.

3 El Corte Inglés
MAP F2 ▪ Avenida António Augusto de Aguiar

The Spanish chain has one of its largest complexes in Lisbon. It includes the city's only true department store, plus restaurants, cinemas and luxury apartments.

4 Parque da Bela Vista
Avenida Gago Coutinho

A large urban park, Bela Vista hosts the Rock in Rio festival, which takes place in even-numbered years.

5 Centro Colombo
MAP B2 ▪ Avenida Lusiada ▪ 10am–midnight daily

Described as the biggest shopping centre in the Iberian peninsula, Colombo has more than 340 shops, plus restaurants and cinemas.

Centro Columbo

6 Estufa Fria
MAP F2 ▪ Parque Eduardo VII

One of the most beautiful botanical attractions in Lisbon, the "Cold Greenhouse" has hundreds of plant specimens from all over the world, and sparkling waterfalls and brooks.

Cartoon in the Museu Rafael Bordalo Pinheiro

7 Museu Rafael Bordalo Pinheiro
MAP C1 ▪ Campo Grande 382 ▪ 218 170 667 ▪ 10am–6pm Tue–Sun ▪ Adm (free until 2pm Sun)

This museum, dedicated to Portugal's best-known caricaturist and ceramic artist, offers a thorough but light-hearted look at Portugal's history.

8 Culturgest
MAP G1 ▪ Rua Arco do Cego ▪ 217 905 155 ▪ 2–7pm Mon, 11am–7pm Tue–Sun ▪ Adm (free Sun)

Housed in the Post-Modern headquarters of a state-owned bank, Culturgest stages music, dance, theatre and exhibitions.

9 Benfica
MAP B2 ▪ Estrada de Benfica

This suburb, now a part of the city, has its own rhythm. The football team did not start here – it moved in – but this is still one of Lisbon's proudest *bairros*.

10 Alameda
MAP G1 ▪ Alameda Dom Afonso Henriques, Avenida Almirante Reis

Alameda's narrow common and its Mussolini-esque lighted fountain offer a glimpse of Lisbon as it was before 1974.

Restaurants and Cafés

PRICE CATEGORIES
For a three-course meal for one with half a bottle of wine (or equivalent meal), taxes and extra charges.

€ under €20 €€ €20–€40 €€€ over €40

1 Laurentina
MAP F1 ■ Avenida Conde de Valbom 71A ■ 217 960 260 ■ €€
The self-proclaimed "King of Cod" offers an exhaustive range of *bacalhau* dishes, along with some meatier options such as pork loin.

2 Ribadouro
MAP K1 ■ Rua do Salitre 2–12 ■ 213 549 411 ■ €€
This is one of the city's best *cervejarias* (beer halls). Like many, it specializes in seafood, although some dishes are a little pricey.

3 Enoteca Chafariz do Vinho
MAP J2 ■ Rua da Mãe d'Água ■ 213 422 079 ■ Closed L; Mon ■ €€
The city's most appealing wine bar serves tasty small dishes to go with its wide choice of wines.

4 Psi
MAP G3 ■ Alameda Santo António dos Capuchos, Jardim dos Sabores ■ 213 590 573 ■ Closed Sun ■ €
This vegetarian restaurant serves dishes from around the world in a pleasant garden setting.

5 SushiCafé Avenida
MAP F3 ■ Rua Barata Salgueiro 28 ■ 211 928 158 ■ Closed Sun ■ €€
One of Lisbon's top Japanese restaurants, SushiCafé specializes in molecular cuisine. Black cod is a favourite ingredient.

6 Café Mexicana
MAP G1 ■ Avenida Guerra Junqueiro 30 ■ €€
This busy café and restaurant in the Guerra Junqueiro/Roma shopping area provides a neat slice of middle-class Lisbon life, along with coffee and ample pastries. The 1960s interior has a certain appeal.

7 Eleven
Lisbon's premier gourmet restaurant, with soft lighting and huge windows overlooking the city, is found at the top of Parque Eduardo VII *(see p43)*. Modern Mediterranean food by Joachim Koerper has earned it a Michelin star *(see p53)*.

Eleven's sophisticated interior

8 Portugália
MAP M2 ■ Avenida Almirante Reis 117 ■ €€
The original – and most would say best – branch of this popular chain. Renowned for its seafood, it also does good steaks and *pregos* (steak sandwiches).

9 Jardim do Torel
MAP L1 ■ Jardim do Torel ■ €€
Set in the 19th-century Jardim do Torel, this café serves light snacks and apéritifs on a terrace with a sweeping panorama. Prices are steeper than average but the location is priceless.

10 Pastelaria Versailles
MAP F1 ■ Avenida República 15A ■ €
Wonderful if slightly yellowed, this café and pastry shop has a grandiose interior, harassed waiters and worldly-wise elderly customers.

See map on p94

TOP 10 The Lisbon Coast

Coastline around Sintra

Its Riviera-rivalling heyday may be a distant memory now, but the varied coastline from the mouth of the Tejo to mainland Europe's westernmost point has other attractions too. Known locally as the *linha*, the coastal region has become one of Lisbon's most populous suburban zones – and yet it retains a laid-back holiday atmosphere. Above and behind it, Sintra's rock-strewn slopes and fragrant woods have a much more ancient ambience.

AREA MAP OF THE LISBON COAST

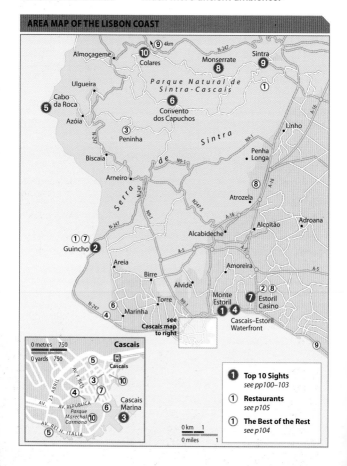

Cascais

0 metres 750
0 yards 750

0 km 1
0 miles 1

- 1 **Top 10 Sights**
  see pp100–103
- 1 **Restaurants**
  see p105
- 1 **The Best of the Rest**
  see p104

1 Monte Estoril

The ridge that separates Estoril from Cascais was the site of the earliest resort development, during the first half of the 20th century. It is now a captivating jumble of grand mansions, shopping arcades and apartment hotels – and still manages to be leafy and quiet in parts. Its railway station is reached by way of a tunnel under the busy *Marginal* coast road.

2 Guincho

Still relatively undeveloped, the windswept coastline beyond Cascais, extending to Cabo da Roca, is exhilarating and scenic, particularly at Guincho. The beach of the same name is popular for surfing (although not recommended for beginners), and the broad sands are good for other beach sports and brisk walks. When it's too windy to swim or sunbathe, head for one of several smaller, more protected beaches on either side. Some of the best restaurants in the area lie along the Guincho road *(see p105)*.

Cascais marina at sunset

3 Cascais Marina

Casa de São Bernardo ▪ 214 824 857 ▪ Reception 9am–8pm Mon–Sat (6pm in winter) ▪ www.mymarina cascais.com

Just beyond the centre of town, and curving around the original fortress on the headland, Cascais Marina has 650 berths and can accommodate yachts up to 36 m (118 ft) long, with a maximum draught of 6 m (20 ft). The many small shops and restaurants also attract a non-sailing crowd. Nearby are the large municipal park of Cascais and the Museu Condes de Castro Guimarães *(see p104)*.

4 Cascais–Estoril Waterfront

Estoril and Cascais are linked by a long promenade that runs just above the beach, but mostly out of sight of the coast road. By far the best walk in either resort, the promenade is lined with small restaurants and bars and occasionally sprayed by Atlantic breakers.

Cascais town and beachfront

5 Cabo da Roca

The westernmost point of mainland Europe is a suitably dramatic clifftop location marked by a lighthouse. Also here is a quotation from Luís de Camões' epic poem *The Lusiads*, carved in stone. The cape is subject to the climatic peculiarities of the whole Sintra region, so take a jumper, even if it's hot when you leave Cascais; temperatures can be 10 degrees lower here, and winds strong. Collectors of memorabilia can buy a certificate to prove that they have walked on the continent's western extremity. There is a good café and restaurant, O Moinho, near the Sintra road turn-off, and Ursa beach *(see p45)* lies just north.

Clifftop Cabo da Roca

6 Convento dos Capuchos

On road EN247-3 ▪ 10am–5pm daily (7pm in summer) ▪ Adm

Standing above Cabo da Roca, near Peninha *(see p104)*, this 16th-century Franciscan monastery is a striking example of monastic frugality, and thus a rarity among Portugal's generally opulent religious buildings. The Capuchin monks' cells are small and plain, hewn from rock and lined with cork against echoes and the cold. The minimal decoration is limited to communal areas such as the chapel, the refectory and the chapterhouse.

COLARES WINE

Once famous for its velvety, long-lived red wines made from the Ramisco grape – one of Europe's few survivors of the phylloxera plague – Colares seems now to be relegated to wine history. Wine is still made, but very little has any of the qualities associated with classic Colares. It seems that the costs of maintaining the old vines – and of planting new ones deep in the sand that protected them from the scourge of the vine louse – is too high.

7 Estoril Casino

Avenida Dr Stanley Ho ▪ 214 667 700 ▪ 3pm–3am daily ▪ Adm varies ▪ www.casino-estoril.pt

Large and rather loud in style, the entertainment heart of Estoril is more than just "Europe's biggest casino", offering both gaming tables and slot machines. It has several good restaurants, an art gallery, a varied concert calendar, a glitzy disco, a theatre stage and titillating floor shows. The palm-lined park in front adds a welcome touch of old-world glamour.

8 Monserrate

These lovely gardens, with their blend of natural and artificial elements, the exotic and the familiar, epitomize some of the essential characteristics of the Sintra region. The artificial "ruin" in the lower garden might have been designed for Walt Disney's *The Jungle Book*, and the rolling lawns are flanked by tropical trees and plants. The Palace

Monserrate Gardens and Palace

(see p32), renovated in 1858 by English nobleman Sir Francis Cook, represents a wonderful pastiche of Portuguese, Arabian and Indian architectural styles.

Palácio Nacional de Sintra

9 Sintra

To have seen the world and left out Sintra is not truly to have seen – thus goes, more or less, a Portuguese saying. When you visit this ravishing hill town, set on the northern slopes of the Serra, it's easy to understand why it was the preferred summer retreat of Portuguese kings (see pp32–3).

10 Colares

This pretty, peaceful village between Sintra and the sea gave its name to one of Portugal's most famous table wines, now made in only tiny amounts of variable quality. (Wine-lovers can visit the cooperative in Colares, at the beginning of the road to Praia das Maçãs, or go out to Azenhas do Mar and look up Paulo Bernardino da Costa, a tenacious producer.) All the same, it's well worth lingering in the older parts of Colares, shaded by plane trees with their peeling, mottled bark. Seek out the restaurant and tea salon Sussegad in the church square, and soak up the old atmosphere of privilege edged by penury.

A SINTRA DRIVE

▶ MORNING

Starting out from **Cascais**, drive along the Guincho coast towards Cabo da Roca (road N247). After Guincho beach, the road begins to climb. Follow the main road past the turning to Malveira da Serra. Turn off to the left for **Cabo da Roca** or, a tiny bit further on, to the right for **Peninha** and **Convento dos Capuchos**. The latter offers opportunities for walks in the woods and views across the Serra; the former an invigorating lungful of sea air and the possibility of a drink at **O Moinho**. Back on the main road, carry on towards **Colares** and stop there for lunch, taking time to explore the village.

AFTERNOON

From Colares take the smaller N375 road heading inland towards Sintra, which will lead you past Eugaria and to **Monserrate**. Make an extended stop at Monserrate, giving yourself time to enjoy the gardens. Carry on along the lovely road that tunnels through the woods until you reach stately **Seteais**, where tea might be in order. A short distance further on you will come to **Quinta da Regaleira** – worth visiting for its gardens and esoterica – before you enter **Sintra** proper. Follow the road up, until you find parking above the main town, then walk down and do the sights or head straight to **Lawrence's** (see p116) for dinner. You can return to Cascais (and Lisbon) via the faster N9.

See map on p100

The Best of the Rest

Parque da Pena and the Palácio

1 Parque da Pena
N247-3 ▪ 10am–6pm (8pm in summer) daily ▪ Adm

The paths in the park around the Palácio da Pena lead to the highest point in the Sintra hills – Cruz Alta, at 530 m (1,740 ft).

2 Golf courses
There are eight golf courses along the Lisbon coast. Most are good, but Penha Longa, between Cascais and Sintra, and Oitavos, in the Quinta da Marinha complex, are the very best places to play.

3 Peninha
N247

The Capela de Nossa Senhora de Penha was built at the turn of the 17th century. In 1918 António Carvalho Monteiro, millionaire owner of the Quinta da Regaleira (see p32), added a mock-fortified eagle's-nest residence.

4 Casa das Histórias Paula Rego
Avenida da República 300, Cascais ▪ 214 826 970 ▪ 10am–6pm (7pm in summer) daily ▪ Adm

The works of the Portuguese artist Paula Rego, known for depictions of folk tales and strong female types, are celebrated here.

5 Boca do Inferno
Estrada da Boca do Inferno (N247-8)

The rocky coastline beyond Cascais is full of crevices cut by the waves.

The "Mouth of Hell" is a particularly deep one, where the waves roar in and then shoot up a vertical hole, creating a geyser-like jet of spray.

6 Citadela de Cascais
Avenida D. Carlos I

The 16th-century ramparts of this impressive fortress enclose several upmarket boutiques and art galleries, as well as a *pousada* which houses the Taberna da Praça restaurant.

7 Cascais Cultural Centre
Avenida Rei Humberto II de Itália 16 ▪ 214 815 660 ▪ 10am–6pm Tue–Sun

Housed in a renovated 17th-century convent building, this centre holds regular exhibitions and concerts.

8 Autódromo do Estoril
N9, Alcabideche

The Formula 1 Portuguese Grand Prix was held at Estoril's racetrack from 1984 to 1996. Today it hosts MotoGP and A1 Grand Prix events.

9 Azenhas do Mar
N375

This clifftop village spills down towards a rock pool by the Atlantic ocean. With several restaurants, it is popular for Sunday lunch outings.

Azenhas do Mar, above a rock pool

10 Museu Condes de Castro Guimarães
Avenida Rei Humberto II de Itália ▪ 214 815 308 ▪ 10am–5pm Tue–Sun ▪ Adm

This tower and grand villa on a small creek just beyond Cascais marina (see p101) are said to have been inspired by a painting.

Restaurants

PRICE CATEGORIES

For a three-course meal for one with half a bottle of wine (or equivalent meal), taxes and extra charges.

€ under €20   €€ €20–€40   €€€ over €40

1 Fortaleza do Guincho
Estrada do Guincho, Cascais ▪ 214 870 491 ▪ €€€

Magnificently sited in a 17th-century fortress, this Michelin-starred restaurant has a modern French menu that features Portuguese ingredients.

2 Estoril Mandarim
Casino do Estoril ▪ 214 667 270 ▪ Closed Mon, Tue ▪ €€

Part of the Casino complex in Estoril, Portugal's most luxurious Chinese restaurant is also its best.

3 Aroma
Rua das Flores 18, Cascais ▪ 214 864 501 ▪ Closed Mon ▪ €€

Come to this colourful restaurant for authentic specialities from India and Thailand, such as roast duck in coconut milk and red curry.

4 Dom Grelhas, Cascais
Casa da Guia, Estrada do Guincho ▪ 214 839 967 ▪ €€

Located in Casa da Guia, a gated huddle of restaurants and shops, Dom Grelhas specializes in grilled meat and fish, with a sea view.

5 O Pereira, Cascais
Travessa da Bela Vista 42, Cascais ▪ 214 831 215 ▪ Closed Thu ▪ €

This small, friendly restaurant serves hearty Portuguese food, prepared in a timeless way.

6 Verbasco, Cascais
Quinta da Marinha Oitavos Golf ▪ 214 860 606 ▪ Closed D daily; closed Mon ▪ €€€

Sophisticated modern cuisine is served here in the airy clubhouse of the Oitavos golf course.

7 Porto de Santa Maria
Estrada do Guincho ▪ 214 879 450 ▪ €€€

Occupying a low, modern building overlooking the dramatic coastline near Guincho beach, Porto de Santa Maria is one of the country's top fish and seafood restaurants.

Freshly caught shellfish at Porto de Santa Maria, on the Guincho coast

8 Four Seasons Grill, Estoril
Hotel Palácio Estoril, Rua Particular ▪ 214 648 000 ▪ Closed L ▪ €€€

This is one of the Lisbon coast's most sophisticated fine-dining venues. Set on a stylish mezzanine and lower floor, it changes its menu and decor according to the seasons.

9 Bar das Avencas
Avenida Marginal, Parede ▪ 214 572 717 ▪ Closed Tue in winter ▪ €

Seemingly hanging off the cliff above a quiet beach, this simple but nicely designed bar offers a menu of sand-wiches, salads and hamburgers, plus a couple of similarly unfussy cooked dishes.

10 O Pescador, Cascais
Rua das Flores 10B, Cascais ▪ 214 832 054 ▪ Closed Mon ▪ €€

Nautical memorabilia adorns the walls of this restaurant, which specializes in fresh seafood. The wine cellar is one of the best stocked in the region.

See map on p100

Streetsmart

Statue of poet Fernando Pessoa outside A Brasileira café in Chiado

Getting To and Around Lisbon

Arriving by Air

Humberto Delgado
airport is on Lisbon's northern outskirts, 7 km (4 miles) from the centre. There are regular flights from the main airports throughout Europe, as well as from the USA. A taxi to the centre costs €15–18 depending on the time of day. Allow 20–30 minutes, or twice that during rush hour. Aerobus Line 1 runs to the riverfront at Cais do Sodré, via the central Avenida da Liberdade, Rossio and Praça do Comércio, every 20 minutes and costs €3.50. Aerobus Line 2 serves the business district around Praça de Espanha, via Sete Rios and Entrecampos. You can also take the metro (change at Alameda for the centre). Single tickets cost €3.50.

Arriving by Rail

Santa Apolónia station is the terminus for regional and high-speed Alfa Pendular trains from northern Portugal and for services from Madrid. Most interregional and local trains from south and east Portugal (except the local Fertagus trains) arrive at Oriente station in the northeast of the city. Trains on this route also stop at Entrecampos in the north of the city. There are regular local connections from Oriente to central Santa Apolónia station, or you can take the metro to one of the more central stops.

Arriving by Coach

Most national and international buses arrive at the main city bus station at Sete Rios, by the zoo. From here it is around 15 minutes to the centre on the Linha Azul metro line. Some services also stop at Oriente station, on the Linha Vermelha line. The main national coach carrier is **Rede Expressos**, which has regular services to most towns and cities throughout the country.

Arriving by Road

You can arrive from the north on the A1, which passes the airport. From the south and east, drivers arrive on the A2 motorway via the 25 de Abril suspension toll bridge. An alternative is to take the A12, which branches off the A2 just after Setúbal and leads to the 17-km (11-mile) Vasco da Gama toll bridge, the best approach for the north and east of the city via the airport.

Getting Around by Metro and Bus

Covering most of the city apart from the west, Lisbon's modern metro network is the fastest way of getting around. Buy tickets at machines by the entrance or at the kiosks, though these are usually unstaffed. Trains run from 6:30am to 1am. Buses run to all parts of the city and are generally reliable, though subject to traffic conditions. Most bus stops display route maps and many have electronic indicators to show when the next bus is due.

Getting Around by Trams and Funiculars

Trams and funiculars are Lisbon's most appealing forms of public transport, but not its most efficient. The most useful tram for seeing the city is the 28, which runs from the Alfama district to Prazeres in the west via the historic centre, and the 25, which runs parallel to the riverfront and serves the area west of the centre. The 15 runs on a modern, fast line from Praça da Figueira to Belém and Algés.

Funiculars carry weary *lisboetas* up several of the city's steepest hills. The most useful ones are the lift-like Elevador da Santa Justa, from the Baixa to Convento do Carmo; Elevador da Glória, from the main Restauradores square to the Bairro Alto; and the two-part Elevador Baixa and Elevador Castelo, from the Baixa to the foot of the castle.

Getting Around by Train

Local trains to the beach resorts of Estoril and Cascais depart from the riverside Cais do Sodré station. Stopping trains go via Belém and Lisbon's docks at Alcântara. Trains to Sintra and Queluz depart from Rossio and Entrecampos stations.

Getting Around by Car

Lisbon's central streets are narrow and frequently congested, so driving is not recommended. There are several central car parks, as well as metered on-street parking, though spaces get snapped up quickly. Most car hire firms have offices at the airport and in central locations, as well as on the coast. All European and US driving licences are valid in Portugal. Drivers must show a valid licence and be aged at least 21.

Getting Around by Taxi

Cream or black-and-green Lisbon taxis may be hailed, caught at ranks or ordered by phone. They are plentiful outside rush hour. Fares are low for Europe. A ride across town should cost around €20. Tourist taxis are unmarked except for a green "A" on the bumper. They charge more and often line up at the airport taxi rank. Tipping is common, usually done by rounding up the fare, for example from €18 to €20.

Getting Around on Foot or by Bike

Central Lisbon is small enough to walk around, though its hills can be hard going, especially in the summer heat.

The cobbled streets and steep slopes usually deter cyclists, though an increasing number of cycle lanes are being provided. The riverside is mostly flat and much of it traffic-free. Take plenty of water, as cycling can be thirsty work in the hot summer months. A good place to hire bikes is on the riverside near Belém.

Getting Around by Ferry

The frequent commuter ferries over the Tejo (departures roughly every 15 minutes) make for a fun excursion to the port suburb of Cacilhas. Ferries depart from Cais do Sodré and cost €1.20 each way. Ferries also run from Belém to Porto Brandão and Trafaria, which have bus services to the Caparica coast.

Buying Tickets and Travel Passes

Individual tickets cost €1.40 for the metro (available from machines by the metro gates), €1.80 for buses, €2.85 for trams and €3.60 for funiculars (valid for two trips). It is cheaper if you buy a rechargeable Viva Viagem card (€0.50), which you can load with amounts from €2 to €15. It then costs just €1.40 for bus and metro journeys. You can also buy a one-day travel pass (€6), which allows unlimited travel on all forms of transport for the day. Viva Viagem cards and travel passes are available from kiosks in the central Praça da Figueira or from any staffed ticket office in the metro, train or ferry stations.

Train tickets can be bought from any main train station and cost just €2.15 one-way to Sintra, Cascais or Estoril.

DIRECTORY

AIRPORT

Humberto Delgado
218 413 500
w ana.pt

AEROBUS
w yellowbustours.com

TRAINS

Comboios de Portugal
707 210 220
351 707 210 220 calls from overseas
(line open 24 hours)
w cp.pt

COACHES

Rede Expressos
707 223 344
w rede-expressos.pt

METRO
w metro.transportes lisboa.pt

BUSES, TRAMS AND FUNICULAR
w carris.transportes lisboa.pt

CAR HIRE

Avis
w avis.com

Budget
w budget.com

Europcar
w europcar.com

Hertz
w hertz.com

Thrifty
w thrifty.com

TAXIS

Cooptáxis
217 932 756
w cooptaxis.pt

Retalis Radio Taxis
218 119 000
w retalis.pt

BIKE HIRE

Belém Bike
w belembike.com

FERRIES
213 500 115
w transtejo.transportes lisboa.pt

Practical Information

Passports and Visas

Visitors from the EU need a valid passport or identity card. Most non-EU nationals can stay for 90 days without a visa but passports must be valid for at least three months beyond their planned departure date. For longer stays, check with a Portuguese embassy or consulate before your trip.

Customs Regulations and Immigration

For EU citizens, there are no limits on goods that can be taken into or out of Portugal, provided they are for your personal use. Outside the EU, you may import the following allowances duty-free: 1 litre of spirits (more than 22 per cent alcohol); two litres of spirits if less than 22 per cent, four litres of wine, 16 litres of beer and 200 cigarettes. Restricted items include fish, and meat and milk from non-EU countries.

Health and Travel Insurance

EU citizens are entitled to free or subsidized medical treatment if they show a European Health Insurance Card (EHIC). Make sure your card has not expired. All other nationalities should take out private health insurance. Report any theft or other crimes to the police and keep a copy of the statement so that you can claim against your insurance.

Travel Safety Advice

Visitors can get up-to-date travel safety information from the **Foreign and Commonwealth Office** in the UK, the **State Department** in the US, and the **Department of Foreign Affairs and Trade** in Australia.

Health

Pharmacies are marked by a green cross and should be the first port of call for minor illnesses. Pharmacy staff often dispense advice as well as medication. A closed pharmacy will have a sign in its window listing one that is open nearby. For more serious problems or emergencies, there are several central public and private hospitals. The largest central hospital is Hospital de Santa Maria.

Personal Security

Lisbon remains a safe city by the standards of most European capitals. Visitors should be wary of pickpockets – particularly on public transport – and should avoid leaving valuables in hired cars. By southern European standards, Portuguese men are respectful of women. However, it pays to be cautious. Walking alone at night through quiet districts – such as the Parque Eduardo VII – is not recommended. There is a police station specifically for tourists on Restauradores, next to the national tourist office in Palácio Foz.

Beach Safety

Beware of currents and undertow at the Atlantic beaches, and don't ignore the safety flags: red – no going in the sea; yellow – no swimming; green – all clear. Nasty stings in shallow water may be from poisonous weever fish (peixe-aranha) buried in the sand. Applying hot water to the area can alleviate the temporary intense pain and swelling; alternatively, seek the help of a lifeguard.

Currency and Banking

Portugal is one of 19 European countries using the euro (€). Euro banknotes come in seven denominations: 5, 10, 20, 50, 100, 200 and 500. There are also eight coins: 1, 2, 5, 10, 20 and 50 cents, and 1 and 2 euros. Major credit cards are widely accepted in bigger hotels, shops, restaurants and bars. The easiest way to withdraw money is using ATMs, known as Multibanco, which are ubiquitous. Nearly all accept debit and credit cards from the major card companies, but transaction charges will apply.

Banks can also be used to change money. For the less common currencies, and outside of banking hours, seek out one of the Forex services in Rossio and Praça da Figueira or one of the city's few money-changing machines, such as the one opposite the Avenida Palace hotel (see p114).

Telephone and the Internet

Portugal has a very modern and efficient mobile telephone network and most mobile phones have good connections throughout Lisbon. The country code is 351.

Wi-Fi is widely available in public spaces, usually for free. There are also several internet cafés, which charge a small fee for timed use, for example **Postnet**.

Postal Services

Correios (post offices) are dotted around the city. For buying stamps, it is more convenient to use the red, coin-operated dispensers, which will save you queuing. Express mail is known as *correio azul*. The main post office on Restauradores is open daily; other post offices operate 9am–6pm on weekdays only.

TV, Radio and Newspapers

Most hotels offer ample choice of international and local TV stations. The state-owned TV company is RTP. RTP 1 is commercial, with various sub-channels, and RTP 2 is culturally oriented. TVI and SIC, which operates a plethora of channels, are private broadcasters. Foreign-language films are subtitled, not dubbed.

On the radio, there is a choice of music stations. Radio Comercial (97.4 FM), Radio Mega Hits (92.4) and Radio Cidade (91.6) play the latest hits. Capital (100.8), RFM (93.2) and Antena 3 (100.3) are all middle of the road. Oxigénio (102.6) and Orbital (101.9) are more dance-oriented, while Antena 2 (94.4) plays classical music.

There are several quality daily newspapers, including *Público* and *Diário de Notícias*, both of which carry cinema listings. The English-language newspaper *The Portugal News* covers Lisbon and Porto.

Opening Hours

Banks are open from 8:30am to 3pm Monday to Friday. Shop hours are from 9am to 1pm and from 2 or 3pm to 7pm on weekdays. Shops are generally open until lunchtime on Saturday and closed all day Sunday. Large shopping centres are an exception, with many outlets staying open all day, every day, until 11pm or midnight.

Most museums and monuments are open Tuesday to Sunday 9:30am–6pm (often later in summer); details are given in the guide.

Restaurants usually open for lunch around noon to 3pm and for dinner from 7 to 11:30pm.

DIRECTORY

EMERGENCY NUMBERS
The emergency number is 112.

PSP Tourism Police
Palácio Foz, Praça dos Restauradores
213 421 623

EMBASSIES

Australian Embassy
MAP F3 ■ Avda da Liberdade 200, 2E, 3rd floor
213 101 500
portugal.embassy.gov.au

Canadian Embassy
MAP F3 ■ Avda da Liberdade 198–200
213 164 600
canadainternational.gc.ca/portugal

UK Embassy
MAP E4 ■ Rua de São Bernardo 33
213 924 000
gov.uk/government/world/portugal

US Embassy
MAP C2 ■ Avda das Forças Armadas1 217 273 300
portugalusembassy.gov

TRAVEL SAFETY ADVICE

Australia
Department of Foreign Affairs and Trade
dfat.gov.au/smartraveller.gov.au/

UK
Foreign and Commonwealth Office
gov.uk/foreign-travel-advice

US
US Department of State
travel.state.gov/

HOSPITALS
Hospital de Santa Maria, Avenida Prof Egas Moniz
217 805 000
chln.min-saude.pt

INTERNATIONAL DIALLING CODES
Portugal + 351
South Africa + 27
UK + 44
USA +1

INTERNET CAFÉS

Postnet
9 Rua Braamcamp, Loja A
213 511 050

Time Difference

Portugal operates on Greenwich Mean Time (GMT), which is four hours ahead of EST. Clocks go forward an hour in late March and back to GMT in late October.

Electrical Appliances

Portugal uses two-pin plugs (220–240 volts). You will need an adaptor, and possibly a transformer (for some US appliances).

When to Go

Lisbon is one of Europe's sunniest capitals, so you can expect sunshine year-round. Spring and autumn are probably the best times to visit, with warm temperatures and fewer crowds, though you should expect the odd shower. June to October is usually clear and hot, with temperatures peaking in July and August. Being on the Atlantic means that the city also gets plenty of rainfall and winter flooding is not uncommon.

Travellers with Special Needs

Disabled visitors will find that the metro is the most accessible form of public transport. Lisbon is hilly and has narrow cobbled pavements with parked cars often blocking the way. Most new buildings offer good disabled access; a lack of facilities elsewhere is often compensated for by a willingness to help.

INR (Instituto Nacional para a Reabilitação) deals with the rights of disabled people, while **Europcar Portugal** rents modified vehicles to mobility-impaired drivers.

Tourist Information

The main Lisbon tourist office is the **Lisbon Welcome Centre** on the riverfront Praça do Comércio. There is also an office in Palácio Foz in Praça dos Restauradores, which has information for Portugal as a whole. Smaller offices can be found at Santa Apolónia train station and at the airport, while Ask Me information kiosks are dotted round the city.

Agenda Cultural is a monthly events and listings mini-magazine in Portuguese. It covers just about everything, is generally accurate – and can be picked up for free at many hotel receptions and tourist attractions. The tourist association's monthly *Follow Me Lisboa* has the fullest coverage of events in English. There are also many helpful tourist websites. Try www.visitportugal.com or www.portugaltravelguide.com.

Trips and Tours

There is a wide range of tours available. **Yellow Bus Tours** offer lots of different tours, including open-top bus tours (daily departures from Praça da Figueira), a hills tram tour (daily departures from Praça do Comércio), a historic tram tour (daily departures from Largo de Camões) and riverboat tours to Belém via Cacilhas (May to October, departures from Terreiro do Paço). Alternatively, take the noisy but fun **Tuk Tuk Lisboa** tours, which run around most of the old town.

Lisbon Walker provides informative and fun walking tours, which vary from walks around the old town to more specifically themed walks. For less effort, you can also take **Segway Tours**.

Dining

It is traditional for the Portuguese to eat out frequently, especially at lunchtime, and as a result you'll find inexpensive places to eat all over the city. These include *tascas* (taverns) and *casas de pasto* (diners), often little more than a simple room serving home cooking. For something more sophisticated, there are countless fine-dining restaurants.

It's worth booking ahead if there's a particular restaurant you have in mind, though most Portuguese don't eat much before 8:30pm, so if you turn up before then there's a good chance you'll get a table, especially during the week. Many places close on Sunday or Monday evenings.

Lisbon, as the capital, hosts restaurants that serve a whole panoply of world cuisine, from African and Brazilian to Indian, Argentinian and Japanese. If you are a vegetarian, you might find that these restaurants offer a broader range of options to choose from. Lisbon is famed for its seafood, and you will find plenty of *marisqueiras*, which are restaurants that specialize in seafood. Another favourite eating spot is the *churrasqueira*, which specializes in chargrilled fish and meat (typically sardines and chicken). Many places offer a very good value *ementa turística*, a three-course set meal that includes a drink.

Traditional menus usually feature grilled meat (lamb, beef, pork and chicken), fantastic fresh fish and seafood, and various stews. *Cozido* is a meat stew, though be aware that it often includes offal. *Caldeirada* is a fish stew, while *cataplana* is similar but served in a metal wok. *Arroz de marisco* is Portugal's version of paella, but soupier, with generous amounts of fish and seafood. With so much fresh fish on the menu, it might seem rather surprising that the national dish is *bacalhau*: salted dried cod. It's served in a variety of ways (there are allegedly 365 ways to cook it), but it is something of an acquired taste.

Not many restaurants have facilities or menus specifically for children, though all will offer half portions and will go out of their way to make children welcome.

It's not usual to give large tips. Most people top up the bill to the nearest round number.

Where to Stay

Lisbon has had a hotel-building boom in recent years, resulting in a wide array of places to stay at competitive rates, especially out of season. Many of the newer hotels are geared to business travellers and lie north of the centre. But there are plenty of options in and around the centre, from simple three-star hotels to boutique and luxury places. Prices can peak at €300 or more for the top hotels in high season, though half that is more usual for most of the year.

Aside from hotels, Lisbon has many inexpensive guesthouses, traditionally known as *pensões* or *residenciais*, but now officially called *alojamentos local*. These are often in traditional buildings in good locations and usually offer en-suite facilities. Expect to pay €80–€100 a night, or as little as €50 for the simplest places, which might just have a sink in the room. Be aware that front-facing rooms can be very noisy. Check to see if they have air conditioning, too, as the city can get very hot in summer.

Lisbon has a number of hostels: official youth hostels and some excellent privately run places. These often have double and family rooms as well as dorms.

There are a few options for self-catering stays, ranging from characterful apartments in the historic Alfama quarter to plush studios in the suburbs.

Lisbon's main camp site is in the Monsanto Park, just outside the city centre. There are several good Oribitur camp sites in the beach resorts around Lisbon.

DIRECTORY

DISABLED VISITORS

Europcar Portugal
Aeroporto de Lisboa
219 407 790.

INR (Instituto Nacional para a Reabilitação)
910 517 886
w inr.pt

TOURIST OFFICES

Lisbon Welcome Centre
MAP M5 ▪ Praça do Comércio/ Rua do Arsenal 15
910 517 886
w visitlisboa.com

Palácio Foz
MAP L2 ▪ Praça dos Restauradores
213 463 314.

Portela Airport
218 450 660.

Santa Apolónia train station
910 517 982

TRIPS AND TOURS

Lisbon Walker
218 861 840
w lisbonwalker.com

Segway Tours
w lisbonsegwaytours.pt

Tuk Tuk Lisboa
213 478 103
w tuk-tuk-lisboa.pt

Yellow Bus Tours
966 298 558
w yellowbustours.com

WHERE TO STAY

Accommodation Booking Sites
w airbnb.com
w booking.com
w hostelworld.com

Youth Hostel and Camp Sites
w lisboacamping.com
w orbitur.pt
w pousasdasjuventude.pt

Places to Stay

Luxury Hotels

Avenida Palace
MAP L3 ▪ Rua 1 de Dezembro 123 ▪ 213 218 100 ▪ www.hotel avenidapalace.pt ▪ €€
The doyen of the city's luxury hotels has a colourful history going back to the early 20th century. Since a major restoration, some purists have found it all a bit too mock-*belle époque*, but the location and atmosphere are hard to beat.

Heritage Avenida Liberdade
MAP F3 ▪ Avenida da Liberdade 28 ▪ 213 404 040 ▪ www.heritage.pt ▪ €€
Part of the small Heritage hotel group, this centrally located hotel occupies a restored late 18th-century building. Portuguese architect Miguel Câncio Martins has retained the building's original features, complementing them with a luxuriously simple, modern boutique-style interior.

Palácio do Governador
MAP A6 ▪ Rua Bartolomeu Dias 117 ▪ 213 007 009 ▪ www. nauhotels.com ▪ €€
Housed in an attractively restored historic building in the tourist centre of Belém, this exquisite hotel has a gourmet restaurant and a spa.

Pestana Palace
MAP C5 ▪ Rua Jau 54 ▪ 213 615 600 ▪ www. pestana.com ▪ €€
Occupying a marvellously restored 19th-century palace with views of the Tejo, this grand hotel has newer extensions framing a garden. It is located between central Lisbon and Belém.

Pousada de Lisboa
MAP M5 ▪ Praça do Comércio 31–34 ▪ 210 407 640 ▪ www.pestana. com ▪ €€
Housed in the former Ministry of Internal Affairs, right on the riverfront Praça do Comércio, this *pousada* combines tradition and modern flair. Plush, elegant rooms, many overlooking the river, are complemented by a sauna, spa, swimming pool, two bars and an excellent restaurant.

Real Palácio
MAP F2 ▪ Rua Tomás Ribeiro 115 ▪ 213 199 500 ▪ www.real hotelsgroup.com ▪ €€
Old and new Lisbon come together here. A restored private palace, dating back to the 17th century in its oldest parts, adjoins a modern hotel building. The latter is filled with reproduction furnishings, but it is the palace, with its small patio, archways and tiled stairwells, that is the highlight.

Sofitel Lisbon Liberdade
MAP K1 ▪ Avenida da Liberdade 127 ▪ 213 228 300 ▪ www.sofitel-lisboa.com ▪ €€
Ideally placed near Lisbon's commercial district and close to the main sights, the stylish Sofitel is popular with business executives for its modern facilities.

Olissippo Lapa Palace
MAP E5 ▪ Rua do Pau da Bandeira 4 ▪ 213 949 494 ▪ www.olissippo hotels.com ▪ €€€
Opulent and eclectic in its decor, this hotel is an established jewel in Lisbon's crown. The location is quiet, but quite a walk from the centre.

Ritz Four Seasons
MAP F3 ▪ Rua Rodrigo de Fonseca 88 ▪ 213 811 400 ▪ www.fourseasons.com/lisbon ▪ €€€
From the outside, the Ritz Four Seasons perhaps isn't much, but it offers characterful interiors and excellent facilities, including a rooftop running track with amazing view of the city. Most importantly, the Ritz provides wonderful hospitality and is absolutely dedicated to its guests.

Character Hotels

Bairro Alto
MAP K4 ▪ Praça Luís de Camões 2 ▪ 213 408 288 ▪ www.bairroaltohotel.com ▪ €€
Set in an attractively restored 18th-century building in Praça de Camões, in the heart of Lisbon, this hotel delivers luxury with style.

Britânia

MAP F3 ▪ Rua Rodrigues Sampaio 17 ▪ 213 155 016 ▪ www.heritage.pt ▪ €€

Situated in a quiet street just off Avenida da Liberdade, the Britânia is housed in a 1940s building, which combines wood and marble in a glorious restoration of its original Art Deco design. Rooms are sleek, tasteful and modern.

Inspira Santa Marta

MAP F3 ▪ Rua de Santa Marta 48 ▪ 210 440 900 ▪ www.inspirahotels.com ▪ €€

Designed (according to Feng Shui principles) as an urban retreat, the four-star Inspira Santa Marta combines a 19th-century façade with an eye-catching minimalist interior. It is committed to sustainability.

Memmo Alfama

MAP P4 ▪ Travessa das Merceeiras 27 ▪ 210 495 660 ▪ www.memmo hotels.com ▪ €€

The first boutique hotel to make an appearance in the historic Alfama district, this has a range of tastefully furnished rooms hidden behind the façade of a gorgeous 19th-century building. You'll also find a wine bar, pool and terrace offering dazzling views across the Tejo estuary.

Solar do Castelo

MAP N3 ▪ Rua das Cozinhas 2 ▪ 218 806 050 ▪ www.solardocastelo. com ▪ €€

Once the kitchens of the original Alcáçovas Palace in Castelo de São Jorge (see pp12–13),

then converted into a private palace in the 18th century, this is now a cozy, eclectically furnished boutique hotel, with rooms around a small courtyard.

Palácio Belmonte

MAP P4 ▪ Páteo Dom Fradique 14 ▪ 218 816 600 ▪ www.palacio belmonte.com ▪ €€€

Eleven suites, each with its own character, occupy the city's oldest private palace, luxuriously restored with wonderful attention to detail and historical authenticity. Buttressed on one side by Castelo de São Jorge (see pp12–13), the Belmonte offers fine views from its terraces, and a small, secluded pool. The place is a dream, but it doesn't come cheap.

Budget Hotels

Florescente

MAP L2 ▪ Rua Portas de Santo Antão 99 ▪ 213 426 609 ▪ www.residencial florescente.com ▪ €

This place feels grander than the price suggests. It is also neater and cleaner than most of its competition. Dead central location, parking facilities and free Wi-Fi enhance the already excellent value it offers.

Globo

MAP K3 ▪ Rua do Teixeira 37 ▪ 213 462 279 ▪ www. anjoazul.com ▪ €

Located on a quiet Bairro Alto street, this basic *pensão* is an economical choice, and very close to 100 Maneiras restaurant (see p83). There is no air conditioning and credit cards are not accepted.

Independente

MAP K3 ▪ Rua São Pedro de Alcântara ▪ 213 461 381 ▪ www.the independente.pt ▪ Dorms €, rooms €€

Part hostel and part quirky hotel, all the rooms here are inside a beautifully restored former mansion. There's a bar and breakfast room, and the adjacent Independente Suites & Terrace has more rooms and a rooftop restaurant.

Lisbon Dreams Guesthouse

MAP F3 ▪ Rua Rodrigo da Fonseca 29 ▪ 213 872 393 ▪ www.lisbondreams guesthouse.com ▪ €

This guesthouse is conveniently located off the Marquês de Pombal roundabout. It has a communal kitchen, an outdoor patio, and a library. The rate includes a buffet breakfast and provides access to Wi-Fi.

Londres

MAP K2 ▪ Rua Dom Pedro V 53, 2 ▪ 213 462 203 ▪ www.pensaolondres. com.pt ▪ €

Longtime favourite of budget travellers, the Londres has gone upmarket. Cheaper rooms are still available, but the best one is at the top, overlooking Bairro Alto's warren of streets.

Traveller's House

MAP M5 ▪ Rua Augusta 89 ▪ 210 115 922 ▪ www. travellershouse.com ▪ €

One of a new breed of high-quality hostels that also offers good-value double rooms. Traveller's House couldn't be more central, occupying a traditional town house on Lisbon's main street.

Rooms with a View

Albergaria Senhora do Monte
MAP P1 ■ Calçada do Monte 39 ■ 218 866 002 ■ www.albergariasenhora domonte.com ■ €€
Set on one of Lisbon's highest hills, this relatively plain hotel boasts some of the city's best views. It's a quiet spot, and full of atmosphere.

Dom Pedro
MAP E3 ■ Avenida Engenheiro Duarte Pacheco 24 ■ 213 896 600 ■ www.dompedro.com ■ €€
This lofty glass pile in the Amoreiras business and shopping district features a luxurious spa and traditionally styled interiors. There are stunning views across the Tejo from almost every room.

Mundial
MAP M3 ■ Praça Martim Moniz 2 ■ 218 842 000 ■ www.hotel-mundial.pt ■ €€
Superbly located in downtown Lisbon, the eight-floor Mundial has views that stretch across the Baixa and up towards the castle. Its comfortable rooms have large windows that open: a potential hazard for young children. The restaurant is popular with local dignitaries.

Sheraton
MAP F2 ■ Rua Latino Coelho 1 ■ 213 120 000 ■ www.sheratonlisboa. com ■ €€
A landmark on the city's modest skyline, the Sheraton has beautiful views and a modern interior. Primarily a business hotel, it offers five-star comfort at reasonable rates and a rooftop restaurant.

Solar dos Mouros
MAP N4 ■ Rua do Milagre de Santo António 6 ■ 218 854 940 ■ www.solardos mouros.com ■ €€
Built over the remains of one of the Moorish-era gates to Castelo de São Jorge, this small hotel has tastefully decorated rooms. Art from the owner's private collection features prominently, as do views of the city and the river.

Tryp Lisboa Oriente
MAP D1 ■ Avenida Dom João II ■ 218 930 000 ■ www.tryporiente.com ■ €€
This modern hotel by Parque das Nações (see pp20–21) offers views of the wide Tejo estuary from its light, airy rooms. Part of the Wyndham Hotels chain, it is handy for the airport.

Altis Belém Hotel & Spa
MAP A6 ■ Doca do Bom Sucesso ■ 210 400 200 ■ www.altis belemhotel. com ■ €€€
Lisbon's first five-star riverfront hotel still commands uninterrupted views of the Tejo. It's also noted for its cutting-edge interior design and its Michelin-starred restaurant, Feitoria.

Lisbon Coast Hotels

Lawrence's
Rua Consiglieri Pedroso 38–40, Sintra ■ 219 105 500 ■ www.lawrences hotel.com ■ €€
Dating from 1764, this charming hotel on the edge of Sintra town claims to be the oldest on the Iberian peninsula. Some of its individually furnished rooms are named after famous guests, among them Lord Byron. The restaurant is run with a real passion.

Senhora da Guia
Estrada do Guincho, Cascais ■ 214 869 239 ■ www.senhoradaguia. com ■ €€
Just outside central Cascais – and close to the Quinta da Marinha golf course – Senhora da Guia embodies civilized luxury. The hotel has a lovely salt-water swimming pool with an adjacent bar.

Albatroz
Rua Frederico Arouca 100, Cascais ■ 214 847 380 ■ www.albatroz hotels.com ■ €€€
Central Cascais' most characterful hotel has a to-die-for location on a promontory with sandy beaches to either side. The main building typifies the summer villas built here for aristocrats in the 19th century.

Farol Design
Avenida Rei Humberto II de Itália 7, Cascais ■ 214 823 490 ■ www. farol.com.pt ■ €€€
Within an extended villa overlooking the sea, this modern luxury hotel has interiors designed by top names in Portuguese fashion. For all the design hype, the main attraction is that some rooms have floor-to-ceiling windows, providing a unique bedtime experience.

Fortaleza do Guincho
Estrada do Guincho, Cascais ▪ 214 870 491 ▪ www.guinchotel.pt ▪ €€€
Housed in an old fortress on a cliff by Guincho beach, this hotel has vaulted rooms and grand staircases. Best of all are the junior suites, with their arcaded terraces facing the Atlantic. The restaurant has one Michelin star.

Palácio Estoril
Rua Particular, Estoril ▪ 214 648 000 ▪ www.palacioestorilhotel.com ▪ €€€
Harking back to Estoril's heyday as a glamorous resort, the Palácio was built in the 1930s and former guests range from royalty to spies. Testament to its enduring grandeur are the hotel's interiors and impeccable service.

Palácio Seteais
Rua Barbosa du Bocage 8–10, Sintra ▪ 219 233 200 ▪ www.tivolihotels.com ▪ €€€
One of the many gems of the Sintra region, this palatial hotel was built in 1787; its Neo-Classical façade and triumphal arch were added later. Now part of the Tivoli chain, it offers all the usual luxuries and an inimitable atmosphere.

Self-catering, Family and Camping

Avenida Park
MAP F2 ▪ Avenida Sidónio Pais 6 ▪ 213 532 181 ▪ www.avenidapark.com ▪ €
Just off Parque Eduardo VII (see p95), this hotel offers good value and a practical location. Most rooms overlook the park.

Camping Orbitur, Costa da Caparica
Avda Afonso de Albuquerque, Quinta S António ▪ 212 901 366 ▪ www.orbitur.pt ▪ €
Situated near the northern end of the Caparica coast, this camp site set among pines is just 200 m (220 yards) from the beach. Many lisboetas have semipermanent set-ups here, and it can get crowded in the summer.

Camping Orbitur, Guincho
Lugar de Areia, Cascais ▪ 214 870 450 ▪ www.orbitur.pt ▪ €
Attractively located among umbrella pines behind the dunes of Guincho beach, this camp site is popular with surfers. Among its facilities is a tennis court. Bungalows are available.

Lisboa Camping
MAP B3 ▪ Estrada Circunvalação ▪ 217 628 200 ▪ www.lisboacamping.com ▪ €
Lisbon's main camp site is located in the Monsanto park (see p86), immediately west of the centre. Well equipped in practical as well as leisure terms, it can get crowded in the summer, particularly at weekends. Those who prefer a solid roof over their heads can rent a bungalow.

Real Residência
MAP F1 ▪ Rua Ramalho Ortigão 41 ▪ 213 822 900 ▪ www.realhotelsgroup.com ▪ €
Comprising 22 suites and two studios, all with kitchenettes, this suite hotel stands just across the street from the Museu Calouste Gulbenkian

(see pp30–31), while Parque Eduardo VII is only a few blocks away. Guests can also access the health club at sister hotel the Real Palácio (see p114), which is located a bit further away.

Roma
MAP K2 ▪ Travessa da Glória 22A ▪ 213 460 557 ▪ www.residencialroma-lisbon.com ▪ €
A pensão residencial, the Roma has 25 rooms and 12 small apartments equipped with kitchenettes. It's a basic place, but sound and clean, and the location is great, just around the corner from the Elevador da Glória (see p79). The apartments are on the third and fourth floors of the building; there is no lift.

VIP Executive Éden Aparthotel
MAP L2 ▪ Praça dos Restauradores 24 ▪ 213 216 600 ▪ www.viphotels.com ▪ €
Housed in what was once the grand Art Deco Eden theatre, overlooking Restauradores, this is Lisbon's most central and well-equipped apartment hotel. The decor is a little dated, but the rooftop pool offers great views over the city.

Clarion Suites
MAP F3 ▪ Rua Rodrigo da Fonseca 44 ▪ 210 046 600 ▪ www.choicehotelseurope.com ▪ €€
This well-equipped mid-range hotel is to be found near the Marquês de Pombal roundabout. Standard suites are small and have kitchenettes. Grander penthouse suites are also available.

For a key to hotel price categories see p114

Index

Acknowledgments

Author

Tomas Tranæus is a travel writer, translator and photographer based in Lisbon. He has contributed to *Eyewitness Portugal* and *Lisbon*, and to the *Time Out* guide to Lisbon. He also writes for Swedish publications.

The author would like to thank Carlos Oliveira for his invaluable assistance, his colleagues at the Portuguese National Tourist Office, London, and the Lisbon Tourist Association, Lisbon.

Additional contributor
Matthew Hancock

Publishing Director Georgina Dee

Publisher Vivien Antwi

Design Director Phil Ormerod

Editorial Kate Berens, Michelle Crane, Sally Schafer, Sophie Wright

Design Tessa Blindloss, Richard Czapnik, Marisa Renzullo

Picture Research Susie Peachey, Ellen Root, Lucy Sienkowska, Oran Tarjan

Commissioned Photography Rough Guides/ Natascha Sturny, Tony Souter, Linda Whitwam, Peter Wilson

Cartography Suresh Kumar, James MacDonald, Casper Morris, Reetu Pandey

DTP Jason Little, George Nimmo

Production Nancy-Jane Maun

Factchecker Mark Harding

Proofreader Susanne Hillen

Indexer Hilary Bird

Illustrator Chapel Design & Marketing

First edition created by Coppermill Books, London

Revisions team
Parnika Bagla, Bhavika Mathur, Lucy Richards

Picture Credits

The publisher would like to thank the following for their kind permission to reproduce their photographs:
Key: a-above; b-below/bottom; c-centre; f-far; l-left; r-right; t-top

100 Maneiras: Fabrice Demoulin 83crb.

123RF.com: joseelias 3tl, 10cla, 60-1; Arseniy Rogov 16-7.

4Corners: Maurício Abreu 96t; Michael Howard 4cla; SIME/Johanna Huber 2tr, 34-5, 88tl; SIME/Paolo Giocoso 12bl.

A Travessa: 91cr.

Alamy Stock Photo: AEP 26cl; age fotostock/ José Antonio Moreno 58b, Juan Carlos Muñoz 78tl, /M&G Therin-Weise 62tl; Paulo Amorim 48t; Mieneke Andeweg-van Rijn 17crb; Art Directors & TRIP ArkReligion.com 68tl; Andrew Duke 10cl; Eric Farrelly 57br; Paul Gapper 46cb, 57tl; GM Photo Images 16cla; Hemis/Anna Serrano 84tr, 85cra; hemis.fr/ Patrice Hauser 82b; Peter Horree 86bl; imageBROKER/Egon Bömsch 40bl; Bjanka Kadic 51cl, 55br; John Kellerman 14crb, 14-5, 15tl; Cro Magnon 39br, 65clb, 80bl, 86tr; dov makabaw 81cla; Miguel Moya 70br; North Wind Picture Archives 36b; James O'Sullivan 4cl; Sean Pavone 1, 59tr, 64b; REDA &CO srl/ Michele Bella 75cr; Mauro Rodrigues 49cl; Sagaphoto.com/Forget Gautier 50b; Roman Sigaev 23tl; M. Sobreira 39cl, 83cl; StockPhotosArt - Urban Landscape/Sofia Pereira 20-1, 79cl; SuperStock/Richard Cummins 16br; Rachel Torres 64tr; Travel Pictures/Pictures Colour Library 69tl, 77cla; Ivan Vdovin 6tr, 12cr, 14cla, 15br, 21tl; Ken Welsh 4t, 11cra, 78cra; Dudley Wood 26-7, 55tl.

Arte Rústica: 72cb.

AWL Images: Mauricio Abreu 21br, 45tr, 58tr; Michele Falzone 13cra.

Bar Lounge: 90tl.

Bica do Sapato: Luisa Ferreira 52tl, 67cl.

Bridgeman Images: 37tr; Gerald Bloncourt 37cl; Stapleton Collection 36tr.

Casa-Museu Fundação Medeiros e Almeida: 94cla, 95t.

Chapitô: 66cl.

Centro Colombo: 98bl.

Confeiteria Nacional: 74cl, João Robalo 53tr.

Corbis: Mauricio Abreu 41tr, 47clb; JAI/Alan Copson 13tl; JAI/Mauricio Abreu 6cr; Frank Krahmer 45cl; Holger Leue 49tr; Sylvain Sonnet 27crb, 77br.

Direção-Geral do Património Cultural/ Arquivo de Documentação Fotográfica(DGPC/ADF): Francisco Arruda/ Luis Pava āoBaluarte 23clb; Museo Nacional dos Coches 38b; Museu Nacional de Antiga 18-9; Museu Nacional de Arte Antiga, Lisboa Instituto dos Museus e da Conservação - MC 10cb, 19crb, 38tl; Museu Nacional do Azulejo/ Luísa Oliveira 2014 27tl.

Doca Piexe: Write View/Paulo Castanheira 91clb.

Dreamstime.com: Allexander 34-5c; Luis Alvarenga 87cl; Leonid Andronov 46bl; Bastabla 63tr; Artur Bogacki 56bl; Olena Buyskykh 101b; Carlos Caetano 44tr; Henner

Damke 41clb; Phil Darby 54br; Dirk123 84cla; Emicristea 69b, 70cl; Rob Van Esch 17tl, 24-5; Europhotos 92-3; Gvictoria 11tl, 22-3; Ideastud 4clb; Joyfull 101tr; Vichaya Kiatying-angsulee 71cla; Martin Lehmann 4crb; Artem Merzlenko 4b, 6cla; Juan Moyano 3tr, 106-7; Sergiy Palamarchuk 70cra; Sean Pavone 42t, 100tl; Antonio Ribeiro 22clb; Arseniy Rogov 102cl; Saiko3p 32-3; Sam74100 43tr, 44b, 46t, 56tl; Rui G. Santos 96b; Jose I. Soto 2tl, 8-9; Stevanzz 95br, 104clb; Rui Vale De Sousa 4cra; Vlat456 103tl; Zts 10bl, 40tr, 54cla, 59cl, 97cla, Zts 74br.

Enoteca de Belém: Fernando Picarra 89crb.

Fundação Calouste Gulbenkian, Lisbon: 11cb, 30clb, 30-1, 31tl, 31ca, 31crb.

Fundação Millennium bcp : Núcleo Arqueológico 56cr.

Hospital de Bonecas: Nick Sinclai 73crb.

Leitão & Irmão: 80ca.

© **Maritime Museum Portugal:** Rui Salta 88c.

Museu da Marioneta: Diogo Ferreira 86cla.

Museu Rafael Bordalo Pinheiro: 98cra.

Parreirinha de Alfama: 51tr.

Pois, Café: Tiago Xavier 66br.

Porto de Santa Maria: 105cra.

Parques de Sintra - Monte da Lua, S.A.(PSML): 32clb; Emigus 11b, 32cla, 33tl, 33crb, 102br; Palácio de Queluz/ Carlos Pombo 11clb; Wilson Pereira 28-9, 29br, 104tl.

Rex by Shutterstock: Lydia Evans 18clb; imageBROKER/Silvana Guilhermino 13bc; Robert Harding/Michael Runkel 43bl.

Robert Harding Picture Library: Andre Goncalves 78b.

Station Restaurant & Club: Matos Fernandes 50tl.

Teatro Nacional Dona Maria II: Ana Paula Carvalho 72tl.

Thema Hotels & Resorts: Eleven 53cla, 99cr.

Cover:
Front and spine: **Alamy Stock Photo:** Sean Pavone.

Back: **Dreamstime.com:** Europhotos.

Pull Out Map Cover:
Alamy Stock Photo: Sean Pavone.

All other images © Dorling Kindersley
For further information see:
www.dkimages.com

| Penguin Random House

Printed and bound in China

First published in Great Britain in 2007 by Dorling Kindersley Limited 80 Strand, London WC2R 0RL

Copyright 2007, 2017 © Dorling Kindersley Limited

A Penguin Random House Company

16 17 18 19 10 9 8 7 6 5 4 3 2 1

Reprinted with revisions 2009, 2011, 2013, 2015, 2017

A CIP catalogue record is available from the British Library.

ISBN 978 0 2412 5397 7

MIX
Paper from responsible sources
FSC™ C018179
www.fsc.org

As a guide to abbreviations in visitor information blocks: **Adm** = *admission charge;* **DA** = *disabled access;* **D** = *dinner;* **L** = *lunch.*

Phrase Book

In an Emergency

Help!	Socorro!	soo-koh-roo
Stop!	Páre!	pahr'
Call a doctor!	Chame um médico!	shahm' ooñ meh-dee-koo
Call an ambulance!	Chame uma ambulância!	shahm' oo-muh añ-boo-lañ-see-uh
Call the police!	Chame a polícia!	shahm' uh poo-lee-see-uh
Call the fire brigade!	Chame os bombeiros!	shahm' oosh bom-bay-roosh

Communication Essentials

Yes	Sim	seeñ
No	Não	nowñ
Please	Por favor/ Faz favor	poor fuh-vor/ fash fuh-vor
Thank you	Obrigado/da	o-bree-gah-doo/duh
Excuse me	Desculpe	dish-koolp'
Hello	Olá	oh-lah
Goodbye	Adeus	a-deh-oosh
Yesterday	Ontem	oñ-tayñ
Today	Hoje	ohj'
Tomorrow	Amanhã	ah-mañ-yañ
Here	Aqui	uh-kee
There	Ali	uh-lee
What?	O quê?	oo keh
Which	Qual?	kwahl'
When?	Quando?	kwañ-doo
Why?	Porquê?	poor-keh
Where?	Onde?	oñd'

Useful Phrases

How are you?	Como está?	koh-moo shtah
Very well, thank you	Bem, obrigado/da.	bayñ o-bree-gah-doo/duh
Where is/are ...?	Onde está/estão ...?	oñd' shtah/ shtowñ
How far is it to ...?	A que distância fica ...?	uh kee dish-tañ-see-uh fee-kuh
Which way to ...?	Como se vai para ...?	koh-moo seh vy puh-ruh
Do you speak English?	Fala inglês?	fah-luh eeñ-glehsh
I don't understand	Não compreendo	nowñ kom-pree-eñ-doo
Could you speak more slowly please?	Pode falar mais devagar por favor?	pohd' fuh-lar mysh d'-va-gar poor fuh-vor
I'm sorry	Desculpe	dish-koolp'

Useful Words

big	grande	grañd'
small	pequeno	pe-keh-noo
hot	quente	keñt'
cold	frio	free-oo
good	bom	boñ
bad	mau	mah-oo
open	aberto	a-behr-too
closed	fechado	fe-shah-doo
left	esquerda	shkehr-duh
right	direita	dee-ray-tuh
straight on	em frente	ayñ freñt'
near	perto	pehr-too
far	longe	loñj'
up	para cima	pur-ruh see-muh
down	para baixo	pur-ruh buy-shoo
early	cedo	seh-doo

late	tarde	tard'
entrance	entrada	eñ-trah-duh
exit	saída	sa-ee-duh
toilets	casa de banho	kah-zuh d' bañ-yoo
more	mais	mysh
less	menos	meh-noosh

Shopping

How much does this cost?	Quanto custa isto?	kwañ-too koosh-tuh eesh-too
I would like ...	Queria ...	kree-uh
I'm just looking	Estou só a ver obrigado/a	shtoh soh uh vehr o-bree-gah-doo/uh
Do you take credit cards?	Aceita cartões de crédito?	uh-say-tuh kar-toinsh de kreh-dee-too
What time do you open?	A que horas abre?	uh kee oh-rash ah-bre
What time do you close?	A que horas fecha?	uh kee oh-rash fay-shuh
This/that one	Este/Esse	ehst'/ehss'
expensive	caro	kah-roo
cheap	barato	buh-rah-too
size	tamanho	ta-man-yoo
white	branco	brañ-koo
black	preto	preh-too
red	vermelho	ver-mehl-yoo
yellow	amarelo	uh-muh-reh-loo
green	verde	vehrd'
blue	azul	uh-zool'
bakery	padaria	pah-duh-ree-uh
bank	banco	bañ-koo
bookshop	livraria	lee-vruh-ree-uh
cake shop	pastelaria	pash-te-luh-ree-uh
chemist	farmácia	far-mah-see-uh
market	mercado	mehr-kah-doo
newsagent	kiosque	kee-yohsk'
post office	correios	koo-ray-oosh

Sightseeing

cathedral	sé	seh
church	igreja	ee-gray-juh
garden	jardim	jar-deeñ
library	biblioteca	bee-blee-oo-teh-kuh
museum	museu	moo-zeh-oo
tourist information office	posto de turismo	posh-too d' too-reesh-moo
bus station	estação de autocarros	shta-sowñ d' oh-too-kah-roosh
railway station	estação de comboios	shta-sowñ d' koñ-boy-oosh

Staying in a Hotel

Do you have a vacant room?	Tem um quarto livre?	tayñ ooñ kwar-too leevr'
room with a bath	um quarto com casa de banho	ooñ kwar-too kah-zuh d' bañ-yoo
shower	duche	doosh
single room	quarto individual	kwar-too een-dee-vee-doo-ahl'
double room	quarto de casal	kwar-too d' kah-zahl'
twin room	quarto com duas camas	kwar-too koñ doo-ash kah-mash
I have a reservation	Tenho um quarto reservado	tayñ ooñ kwar-too re-ser-vah-doo

Eating Out

Have you got a table for ...?	Tem uma mesa para ... ?	tayñ oo-muh meh-zuh puh-ruh
I want to reserve a table	Quero reservar uma mesa	keh-roo re-zehr-var o-muh meh-zuh
The bill, please	A conta por favor/ faz favor	uh kohn-tuh poor fuh-vor/ fash fuh-vor
I am a vegetarian	Sou vegetariano/a	Soh ve-je-tuh-ree-ah-noo/uh
the menu	a lista	uh leesh-tuh
wine list	a lista de vinhos	uh leesh-tuh de veeñ-yoosh
glass	um copo	ooñ koh-poo
bottle	uma garrafa	oo-muh guh-rah-fuh
knife	uma faca	oo-muh fah-kuh
fork	um garfo	ooñ gar-foo
spoon	uma colher	oo-muh kool-yair
plate	um prato	ooñ prah-too
breakfast	pequeno-almoço	pe-keh-noo-ahl-moh-soo
lunch	almoço	ahl-moh-soo
dinner	jantar	jan-tar
starter	entrada	eñ-trah-duh
main course	prato principal	prah-too prin-see-pahl'
dessert	sobremesa	soh-bre-meh-zuh
rare	mal passado	mahl' puh-sah-doo
medium	médio	meh-dee-oo
well done	bem passado	bayñ puh-sah-doo

Menu Decoder

açorda	uh-sor-duh	bread-based stew
açúcar	uh-soo-kar	sugar
água mineral	ah-gwuh mee-ne-rahl'	mineral water
com gás	koñ gas	sparkling
sem gás	sayñ gas	still
alho	al-yoo	garlic
amêijoas	uh-may-joo-ash	clams
arroz	uh-rohsh	rice
atum	uh-tooñ	tuna
azeitonas	uh-zay-toh-nash	olives
bacalhau	buh-kuh-lyow	dried, salted cod
batatas	buh-tah-tash	potatoes
batatas fritas	buh-tah-tash free-tash	French fries
bica	bee-kuh	espresso
bife	beef	steak
bolo	boh-loo	cake
borrego	boo-reh-goo	lamb
café	kuh-feh	coffee
camarões	kuh-muh-roysh	large prawns
caranguejo	kuh-rañ-gay-joo	crab
carne	karn'	meat
cebola	se-boh-luh	onion
cerveja	sehr-vay-juh	beer
chouriço	shoh-ree-soo	red, spicy sausage
cogumelos	koo-goo-meh-loosh	mushrooms
fiambre	fee-añbr'	ham
fígado	fee-guh-doo	liver
frango	frañ-goo	chicken
frito	free-too	fried
fruta	froo-tuh	fruit
gambas	gam-bash	prawns
gelado	je-lah-doo	ice cream
gelo	jeh-loo	ice
grelhado	grel-yah-d	grilled
maçã	muh-sañ	apple
manteiga	mañ-tay-guh	butter
mariscos	muh-reesh-koosh	seafood
ostras	osh-trash	oysters
ovos	oh-voosh	eggs
pão	powñ	bread
pastel	pash-tehl'	cake
pato	pah-too	duck
peixe	paysh'	fish
pimenta	pee-meñ-tuh	pepper
polvo	pohl'-voo	octopus
porco	por-coo	pork
queijo	kay-joo	cheese
sal	sahl'	salt
salada	suh-lah-duh	salad
salsichas	sahl-see-shash	sausages
sopa	soh-puh	soup
sumo	soo-moo	juice
tamboril	tañ-boo-ril'	monkfish
tomate	too-maht'	tomato
vinho branco	veeñ-yoo brañ-koo	white wine
vinho tinto	veeñ-yoo teeñ-too	red wine
vitela	vee-teh-luh	veal

Numbers

0	zero	zeh-roo
1	um	ooñ
2	dois	doysh
3	três	tresh
4	quatro	kwa-troo
5	cinco	seeñ-koo
6	seis	saysh
7	sete	set'
8	oito	oy-too
9	nove	nov'
10	dez	desh
11	onze	oñz'
12	doze	doz'
13	treze	trez'
14	catorze	ka-torz'
15	quinze	keeñz'
16	dezasseis	de-zuh-saysh
17	dezassete	de-zuh-set'
18	dezoito	de-zoy-too
19	dezanove	de-zuh-nov'
20	vinte	veent'
21	vinte e um	veen-tee-ooñ
30	trinta	treeñ-tuh
40	quarenta	kwa-reñ-tuh
50	cinquenta	seen-kweñ-tuh
60	sessenta	se-señ-tuh
70	setenta	se-teñ-tuh
80	oitenta	oy-teñ-tuh
90	noventa	noo-veñ-tuh
100	cem	sayñ
101	cento e um	señ-too-ee-ooñ
200	duzentos	doo-zeñ-toosh
300	trezentos	tre-zeñ-toosh
400	quatrocentos	kwa-troo-señ-toosh
500	quinhentos	kee-nyeñ-toosh
700	setecentos	set'-señ-toosh
900	novecentos	nov'-señ-toosh
1,000	mil	meel'

Time

one minute	um minuto	ooñ mee-noo-too
one hour	uma hora	oo-muh oh-ruh
half an hour	meia-hora	may-uh-oh-ruh
Monday	segunda-feira	se-goon-duh-fay-ruh
Tuesday	terça-feira	ter-sa-fay-ruh
Wednesday	quarta-feira	kwar-ta-fay-ruh
Thursday	quinta-feira	keen-ta-fay-ruh
Friday	sexta-feira	say-shta-fay-ruh
Saturday	sábado	sah-ba-doo
Sunday	domingo	doo-meen-goo

Lisbon Street Index